Praise for *Staying Online: How to Navigate Digital Higher Education*

"For many years I have enjoyed reading Bob Ubell's essays on online and digital education for their unique and insightful takes on important issues in online learning. I particularly appreciate his ability to shine a light on critical issues in engaging and accessible language. Ubell revisits and expands on many of his ideas in *Staying Online*, while including essential new chapters on remote learning in response to the pandemic and how his views have changed over time. The result is very much more than the sum of its parts. This volume is a must-read for all educators involved with online learning—which, these days, is all educators."

—Karen Swan, Stukel Professor of Educational Leadership at
University of Illinois Springfield, USA

"This collection of relevant chapters about online learning are essential readings and highly recommended for higher education leaders and faculty today. Bob Ubell has been a prominent and distinguished thought leader in the field for more than two decades. His insight and vision provide important guidance to our colleges and universities during this critical period."

—Eric E. Fredericksen, Associate Vice President for
Online Learning at University of Rochester, USA

"Digital higher education has a rich history and is often misunderstood. In this useful, contemporary collection of perspectives built on his extensive experience as an industry pioneer, Bob Ubell traces how online learning is evolving—with an eye toward the inevitable future where digital education is not a novelty but is instead a central, integrated aspect of how higher education institutions operate."

—Sean Gallagher, Executive Director of the Center for
the Future of Higher Education & Talent Strategy
at Northeastern University, USA

Praise for *Going Online: Perspectives on Digital Learning*

"This well-structured, well-researched collection gets to the root of the world's skepticism about digital education, and snippets of humor make it a more entertaining volume than readers might initially expect. Collectively, the essays argue that, despite our misgivings, online education is the best tool for advancing, creating, and distributing knowledge in the modern world."

—Alex Moore, in *TD Magazine* (May 1, 2017)

"Ubell's proposition is that online learning lets students process information in their own time. They can take part in online discussions and ask questions anonymously, without losing face. This demands a new pedagogy—teaching, learning and assessment for active learning communities. Academics must work with web designers and educational technologists to create conditions that let students control the pace and delivery of learning, yet continually share and respond to others' ideas . . . Those shifts can also foster an excitement that Robert Ubell's *Going Online* captures."

—Mike Sharples, Emeritus Professor of Educational Technology
in the Institute of Educational Technology at The Open University, UK,
in *Nature* 540, 340 (December 15, 2016)

"Ubell describes in detail how new technology allows us to use online learning in new ways that are both more participatory and more effective. These assertions come from someone with a remarkable track record of making learning actually happen."

—Ralph Gomory, Research Professor in the Leonard N. Stern School
of Business at New York University, USA, and former President
of the Alfred P. Sloan Foundation

Staying Online

In *Staying Online*, one of our most respected online learning leaders offers uncommon insights into how to reimagine digital higher education. As colleges and universities increasingly recognize that online learning is central to the future of post-secondary education, faculty and senior leaders must now grapple with how to assimilate, manage, and grow effective programs. Looking deeply into the dynamics of online learning today, Robert Ubell maps its potential to boost marginalized students, stabilize shifts in retention and tuition, and balance nonprofit and commercial services. This impressive collection spans the author's day-to-day experiences as a digital learning pioneer, presents pragmatic yet forward-thinking solutions on scaling-up and digital economics, and prepares managers, administrators, provosts, and other leaders to educate our unsettled college students as online platforms fully integrate into the mainstream.

Robert Ubell is Vice Dean Emeritus of the Tandon School of Engineering at New York University and Senior Advisor at Stevens Institute of Technology. The author of *Going Online*, a companion collection to this book, he is a Fellow of the Online Learning Consortium, a columnist at *EdSurge*, and a recipient of the highest honor given for individual achievement in digital education, the A. Frank Mayadas Leadership Award.

Staying Online

How to Navigate Digital Higher Education

Robert Ubell

NEW YORK AND LONDON

First published 2022
by Routledge
605 Third Avenue, New York, NY 10158

and by Routledge
2 Park Square, Milton Park, Abingdon, Oxon, OX14 4RN

Routledge is an imprint of the Taylor & Francis Group, an informa business

© 2022 Taylor & Francis

The right of Robert Ubell to be identified as author of this work has been asserted by him in accordance with sections 77 and 78 of the Copyright, Designs and Patents Act 1988.

All rights reserved. No part of this book may be reprinted or reproduced or utilised in any form or by any electronic, mechanical, or other means, now known or hereafter invented, including photocopying and recording, or in any information storage or retrieval system, without permission in writing from the publishers.

Trademark notice: Product or corporate names may be trademarks or registered trademarks, and are used only for identification and explanation without intent to infringe.

Library of Congress Cataloging-in-Publication Data
A catalog record for this title has been requested

ISBN: 978-0-367-46210-9 (hbk)
ISBN: 978-0-367-47745-5 (pbk)
ISBN: 978-1-003-03632-6 (ebk)

Typeset in Warnock Pro
by Apex CoVantage, LLC

For my daughters, Jennifer and Elizabeth

ALSO BY ROBERT UBELL

Going Online: Perspectives on Digital Learning

Virtual Teamwork: Mastering the Art and Practice of Online Learning and Corporate Collaboration (editor)

Contents

Preface　　*xiii*
Acknowledgments　　*xvii*

Section 1
Emergency Online Learning　　1

1　We Are All Online Learners Now　　3

Section 2
Theory and Practice　　15

2　Theory and Practice　　17

3　Online as an Ethical Practice　　32

4　Adaptive Learning　　42

Section 3
Scaling-up　　49

5　Academic Digital Economy　　51

6　Outsourcing vs. Insourcing　　80

7　MOOC Invasion　　93

xii **Contents**

8 Going Online Abroad 108

9 Finding and Keeping Online Learners 117

Section 4
Problems and Considerations 125

10 Online Cheating 127

11 Online Predators 131

12 Accreditation Works 138

Section 5
Changing My Mind 143

13 Changing My Mind 145

Index *153*

Preface

After I stepped down as vice dean of online learning at New York University's (NYU's) Tandon school of Engineering a few years ago, to my surprise I returned to journalism, a profession I'd occupied quite some time ago, soon after graduating from college. Once again, I found myself—as in my youth—writing for general and specialist periodicals, but instead of covering science, health, and a miscellany of odd subjects as I did then, I now write about the field I've been engaged in for more than two decades—online higher education.

Mostly drawn from my previously published essays in *EdSurge, Inside Higher Ed* and other sources over the last several years, the chapters in this volume stitch them together under collective themes central to online learning in higher education. Most assemble two or more, linking and extending them with longer, more discursive assessments. A few chapters reprint some articles largely as they first appeared. A good part of the opening chapter on the pandemic and the closing one, reconsidering positions I once held but now no longer seem to exert the same force, were written expressly for this volume.

While they cover a number of compelling questions facing virtual instruction today, the aim of these extended essays is to explore which virtual practices are likely to be best for students, increasingly tossed unwittingly into unfamiliar digital academic environments. All have been updated and include more recent material to give shape and substance to earlier pieces requiring broader current perspectives.

The collection is divided into five parts dealing with some of the most pressing challenges faced by online learning in higher education. The first covers virtual instruction in the devastating pandemic, looking back at how colleges and universities responded under the most severe conditions they have ever faced and recalling the troubling consequences of COVID-19 for students and faculty. The second, on theory and practice, opens with how my experience teaching online was influenced by constructivist learning theory. It also covers how digital education affects nontraditional students, focusing on the lack of online student services provided to remote students.

xiv Preface

It closes with a brief overview of the adaptive learning marketplace and what personalized digital education means for struggling students.

Part III, "Scaling-up," shifts from student and faculty perspectives to institutions, exploring how some have come to terms with adopting digital education, with chapters on the vast differences between on-campus and online economies, why some colleges feel compelled to outsource remote learning to commercial vendors, what drives universities to partner with massive online delivery (MOOC) providers, how international students are affected by virtual instruction, and how powerful digital recruitment campaigns are transforming colleges and universities.

Part IV includes three brief chapters covering a variety of serious topics, almost exactly as they first appeared, on how to mitigate cheating online, why accreditation in the U.S. is an admirable democratic practice, and how the Trump administration encouraged for-profit schools to continue their shameless betrayal of vulnerable students. The final section, "Changing My Mind," revisits my earlier doubts about streaming videos and MOOCs, with more generous and accepting reappraisals.

This rough outline, however, merely presents a parallel overview of what you'll find in the table of contents, the grid on which chapters hang, but overlooks troubling underlying currents that crisscross it along a more distressing axis—conflicts that often shake the faculty, disrupt university leadership, and agitate relationships among various campus players. Few other departures from customary academic practice have rattled higher education with such clashing force. Online education has pitted faculty against faculty in fierce battles over quality and efficacy, with traditional professors defending the historic legitimacy of face-to-face instruction against digital interlopers threatening to overturn a thousand years of conventional classroom education. At some colleges, marketing teams, unhappy with online competition threatening their on-campus programs, move digital degrees to the back of the line. Trustees at some schools quarrel with academic leadership over failure to launch online programs more aggressively. Online and on-campus camps often battle over the allocation of already depleted resources.

Conflicts also emerge over which academic unit is responsible for running online programs. Since online learning requires digital acumen, information technology commonly believes its technical expertise gives it the authority. At other schools, teaching and learning centers feel their pedagogical insights give them the requisite knowledge. At still other colleges, no central body runs digital learning, with each academic school managing its own online delivery, as at NYU. At many universities, online units grew out of distance-learning departments, often housed in schools of professional studies, where many digital education operations still reside. But as online practice matured, the provost's office often stepped in, ending internecine skirmishes by taking over virtual education, paralleling its usual role in conventional instruction.

Luckily, these contests never escalated into a national crisis, except when the Obama administration entered a relentless campaign against predatory Wall Street-financed for-profits. Otherwise, on-campus and online rivals have largely settled into a truculent armistice, allowing them to go their separate ways—but also occasionally joining forces in hybrid programs. In my time as online dean, I engaged in battles over reluctance to fund digital recruitment, claims that online classes steal students from on-campus degrees, and other, often climactic but occasionally quite comic, disputes.

Some chapters are drawn from my own experience at Stevens Institute of Technology, New York University, and elsewhere. "Theory and Practice," for example, emerged from a semester teaching online at The New School, a liberal arts college in Manhattan. "Accreditation Works" was drawn from participating as a member of a Middle States Commission on Higher Education team at Rutgers University. Throughout, I weave in my personal narrative when my engagement and perceptions may illuminate my train of thought. Sometimes, serving on a faculty committee or an advisory board, can reveal how powerful cultural norms prevent institutions from being open to change. In one example, in a chapter on nontraditional students, I relate an episode as a member of a university-wide committee that repeatedly failed to address online student services as an essential feature of delivering quality online education, finally empowering a subcommittee to acknowledge the problem. It met once, recognized the need, but never met again.

Most observers imagine that all that's required to go online is to place an instructor in front of a camera or before a webcam. If nothing else, this collection reveals how radically innocent that view is. Across the globe, online learning is a giant machine with many moving parts. In addition to well-trained digital instructors, expert instructional designers, savvy videographers, and skilled techies, operating an online enterprise requires a long and complex chain of other professionals in marketing and recruitment, remote student support services, budgeting and finance, and dozens of other crafts that contribute to making the digital learning engine run.

This is a companion volume to my earlier work, *Going Online*, published in 2017. In merely six years, many things have changed—some quite momentous—especially when all of academia moved online during the pandemic last year, a feat that could not have been achieved earlier. As you

xvi Preface

go through these chapters, you will find other pivotal changes that have contributed to recognizing that digital education is no longer in early formation, as the title of my previous collection suggested, but is here for the long-haul, staying online.

Robert Ubell
New York, February 2021

Acknowledgments

My first encounter with online learning goes back nearly a quarter of a century to its early days when I had just found a position at Stevens Institute of Technology, an engineering school in Hoboken, NJ, as head of what was then quaintly called "web-based distance learning." Soon afterward, an e-mail invited me to attend a meeting of faculty and staff at local universities who had already launched or were contemplating introducing online academic programs.

About two dozen of us showed up at a stylish Manhattan townhouse for talks given by experts sponsored by the Alfred P. Sloan Foundation on what the grant-making institution was then calling "asynchronous learning networks," an idiosyncratic antecedent to what is now commonly known as online learning. Just starting out in my online career, I was unaware that the foundation was encouraging colleges and universities to experiment with digital degrees, among the very first in the nation.

As we were milling about afterwards, a Sloan Foundation officer approached me, introducing himself as Frank Mayadas, the head of Anytime, Anywhere Learning, a relatively new initiative that offered grants to institutions willing to take a stab at virtual education. Frank was eager to learn what I was up to.

"Just about to launch a handful of engineering master's on the web," I responded, uneasy at what suddenly seemed an absurdly ambitious task.

With an eager, broad smile, Frank wondered whether I might be free the following week to meet him at an Indian lunch spot near Rockefeller Center where the Sloan Foundation is located. Over naan and tandoori chicken, he encouraged me to go ahead with an online master's in telecommunications management with a modest Sloan grant.

Thrilled, I took a PATH commuter train under the Hudson River from Manhattan to Hoboken, dashing excitedly into my boss's office at Stevens with my good news. Dismissing what he thought was my academic naivete, he waved his arm scornfully, "No one gets a grant over lunch."

After that fateful Indian buffet, Frank was at my side over the next couple of decades, supporting additional Stevens online degrees, research projects, local conferences, and countless delightful Indian lunches. After the

xvii

xviii   Acknowledgments

foundation's online unit was spun-off, Frank took on the post as president of the Online Learning Consortium (OLC), the premier online learning professional society, successor to the Sloan Consortium, the organization that had previously run annual online learning conferences, now managed by OLC.

Frank's colleague, the noted economist Ralph Gomory, very early recognized the potential of virtual education in higher education, and as president of the foundation, initiated major support for digital education, eventually giving $75 million to colleges and universities across the country to test it. Without the Sloan Foundation, and later OLC, online learning might never have achieved its present remarkable global diffusion. We all owe Ralph and Frank our deepest gratitude for their insight and determination.

Perhaps best of all, for a number of years at the turn of this century, the foundation funded a series of mini thinktanks at Lake George in upstate New York, attended by thirty invited participants. I was lucky to be among those who were exposed to unconventional pedagogical ideas during three-day sessions where the digital learning avant-garde delivered incisive presentations on what ultimately emerged as online best practices. The bright, young pioneers at Lake George are now among the nation's notable leaders in virtual instruction as practitioners and scholars, holding distinguished senior posts at the nation's colleges and universities.

I am profoundly indebted to my mentors and friends who led the way at Lake George and elsewhere; among many others are Meg Benke, SUNY Empire State College; Ed Borbely, University of Wisconsin; Andy DiPaolo, Stanford University; Eric Fredericksen, University of Rochester; Steven Goss, Manhattan College; Joel Hartman, University of Central Florida; Anthony Picciano, City University of New York; Janet Poley, University of Nebraska; Peter Shea, SUNY University at Albany; Jeff Seaman, Babson College; and Karen Swan, University of Illinois.

At Stevens and NYU, I was fortunate to work closely with many gifted colleagues who, because of their special talent in digital education and related skills, were my coaches and advisors, not only during the time we worked together, but long afterward, even today as friends. My warmest appreciation goes to Sebastien Auguste, Briana Bates, Earl Co, Marlene Leekang, Peggy McCready, Neil Rader, Evan Silberman, Kristen Sosulski, Katepalli Sreenivasan, and Jay VanDerwerken. I am especially grateful to Lisa Bellantuono for alerting me to life-cycle recruitment; John Vivolo for championing instructional design; and Robert Zotti for calling my attention to virtual teamwork.

Since stepping down as online dean at NYU's Tandon School, I've had the privilege of consulting for several colleges and online vendors, among them Coursera, The New School, NYU's Wagner School, LIM, Beacon Education, and Stevens Institute of Technology, in addition to serving on McGraw Hill's Learning Science Advisory Board. In these appointments, I've had the exceptional opportunity of collaborating with faculty and senior leaders; among them are Costas Chassapis, Thomas D'Aunno, Kimberly Barletta, Alfred Essa, Robert Feldman, Michael Frank, Susan Gouijnstook, Charles Iannuzzi, Ilan Jacobsohn, Tanya Joosten, Richard Larsen, Carlo Lipizzi, Jeff Maggioncalda, Allison Ruppino, and Lisa Springer.

To support my conclusions, in addition to consulting the published literature and navigating the internet, I reached out to trusted authorities whose opinions are quoted in this book. I extend my deep appreciation for sharing their views to Lisa Bellantuono, Nelson Baker, Zhenghao Chen, Michael Crow, Thomas D'Aunno, Andy DiPaolo, Alfred Essa, Eric Fredericksen, Lev Gonick, Joel Hartman, Phil Hill, Ilan Jacobsohn, Daphne Koller, Rick Levin, Peggy McCready, Shawn Miller, Karen Pollack, Jeff Seaman, Anju Sharma, Peter Shea, Karen Swan, John Vivolo, and Allan Weisberg.

I am thoroughly indebted to Elaine Cacciarelli, who has worked closely with me on numerous projects over many years. For *Staying Online*, besides gathering permissions from original sources, she read and reviewed each chapter with a practiced eye and astute sensitivity.

Grateful appreciation goes to my editor, Daniel Schwartz, who has been a close colleague and guide throughout the process, and to Sathish Mohan and his staff for carefully moving the book through production.

I am especially grateful to my friends—some go all the way back to childhood—whose support and affection eased the challenge of drawing this book together: Robert Benton, Clinton Cowels, Hal Espo, Isabel Freeman, Martha Gever, Rebecca Harrington, James Holmes, Adam Kaplan, Alice Klein, Andrea Marquez, Sandra Mazur, Robert Millner, Nadja Millner-Larsen, Roy Moskowitz, Yvonne Rainer, Ann Reynolds, Gerard Roman, Florence Rowe, Judith Rubin, Neil Salzman, Sheila Slater, Jon Smit, Stephen Stanczyk, and Seymour Weingarten.

I am deeply moved by my family's love and support. My warmest devotion to my daughters Jennifer and Elizabeth, to whom this book is dedicated, and my grandchildren Benjamin, Ella, and Fordon; and to Bryn, Jack, Marielle, Matt, Naiyah, Shane, Steve, and Thornton; to my brothers and stepsisters and their families, Alvin and Sara, Estella and Ernesto, Seymour and Marsha, Anne, and Evelyn. A special happy recognition goes out to grandson Ben for suggesting the *à propos* title, *Staying Online*.

My love for Rosalyn makes it all possible.

* * *

xx Acknowledgments

Most chapters in this collection are drawn from articles published previously over several years in a handful of online and print periodicals. Working in close collaboration with gifted editors sharpened my drafts, turning them into far more accessible and creditable texts. I am especially grateful to editors Jean Kumagai at *IEEE Spectrum*, Doug Lederman at *Inside Higher Ed*, Scott Moore at *TD*, and Jeff Young at *EdSurge* for their fine judgement and gracious flexibility. My appreciation also goes out to the publishers for permission to include extended and updated versions of these articles:

EdSurge

How Online Education Went from Teaching Reform to Economic Necessity for Colleges, March 5, 2020

Why the Convenience University Will Rule Higher Ed, January 13, 2020

Higher Ed Has Now Split into Dual Economies: Online and Traditional, November 6, 2019

Coupling Recruitment with Retention Can Drive up Graduation Rates, September 18, 2019

How Online Degrees Can Advance Worker Careers in a Shifting Economy, August 5, 2019

For Colleges, Outsourcing the Virtual Future Is a Bad Idea, April 22, 2019

Online Learning's "Greatest Hits," February 20, 2019

Can Online Learning Help Higher Ed Reverse Its Tuition Spiral? December 13, 2018

Does Online Education Help Low-income Students Succeed? July 17, 2018

How Risk-averse Universities Take Chances with Satellite Campuses Abroad, May 15, 2018

Will Online Ever Conquer Higher Ed? January 18, 2018

How Online Can Save Small, Private Colleges from Going Under, November 21, 2017

Acknowledgments xxi

Inside Higher Ed

Why Online Is an Ethical Practice, April 10, 2019

From Anxious Online Dean to Confident Virtual Instructor, October 17, 2018

An Inside Look at Why Accreditation Works, June 14, 2018

For State Universities, Big Is In, December 6, 2017

Why Did Harvard Go Outside to Go Online? October 4, 2017

Return of the Online Predators, August 30, 2017

There's No Success Like Failure, July 19, 2017

MOOCs Find Their Sweet Spot, April 12, 2017

Let's End the War between Online and On-campus Instruction, March 22, 2017

Why Online Costs Less, Not More, March 8, 2017

Opportunity for Online Learning, March 1, 2017

Online Cheating, February 6, 2017

IEEE Spectrum

How Online Learning Kept Higher Ed Open During the Coronavirus Crisis, May 13, 2020

Why Your Next Job Training Course May Be a MOOC, February 6, 2017

What Do Employers Really Think of Online Degrees, January 30, 2017

Can MOOCs Cure the Tuition Epidemic? January 23, 2017

How the Pioneers of MOOCs Got It Wrong, January 16, 2017

xxii   Acknowledgments

McGraw Hill

Shaking-up Piggy Bank Minds, November 1, 2018

TD

Making the Most of MOOCs, October 5, 2017

Section 1
Emergency Online Learning

1

We Are All Online Learners Now

Steering the giant lifeboat of academia from on campus to online in just a few weeks in the spring of 2020 has to count as one of the most unimaginable and exceptional feats ever achieved in higher education. Before the COVID-19 pandemic, only a third of U.S. college students were enrolled in online classes (Ubell, 2019b). Suddenly, nearly all of them were.

Under the threat of mass infection and with little or no preparation or planning, millions of professors and instructors around the world shifted their lectures, seminars, discussion sessions, and other in-person classes to online learning platforms. And millions of college students followed them.

Take a look at the following graph, created by noted edtech trend-spotter Phil Hill, illustrating the magical crossing in which U.S. higher education leaped almost entirely online (Hill, 2020a).

The COVID-19 pandemic forced U.S. colleges and universities to move courses online in a matter of weeks. As the rapidly climbing line shows, moving swiftly to the upper right corner in the graph, by the time U.S. campuses closed their gates on or around March 30, 2020, nearly all undergraduate and graduate courses had switched online.

Nothing in the history of higher education prepared our academic institutions to act with such uncanny speed. Similar moves occurred in Europe and Asia, but only in advanced economies was the transformation as swift as in the United States. For faculty and students in less developed countries,

4   Emergency Online Learning

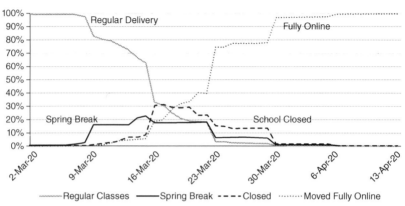

FIGURE 1.1 Percentage of US higher ed institutions moving to fully online delivery of traditional face-to-face courses during COVID-19 crisis
Source: Phil Hill/MindWires

where internet service is poor or lacking and many don't have digital devices, shifting online has not been nearly as swift or as easy.

In nonpandemic times, even the most modest change at a college or university can take months, if not years. Think of the committees, reports, reviews, and approvals needed to introduce even a timid curriculum revision. That millions of faculty members moved hundreds of thousands of courses online in a matter of weeks reveals the surprising resilience of academia in crisis.

In a breathtaking reversal, professors totally abandoned their familiar campus for an alien virtual world, suddenly dropping opposition to digital education. Fierce resistance dissolved practically overnight, with hardly anyone calling on institutions to stop their headlong plunge online. It was as if the university was on fire, with faculty rushing with digital buckets before the place burned down. Putting up a fight was useless. Defiance collapsed quickly, with hardly anyone raising a hand to stop it because there was no other way. Either go online—or close down the university.

Anju Sharma, an associate teaching professor of chemistry and chemical biology at Stevens Institute of Technology in Hoboken, N.J., had never taught online. Then, on Monday, March 9, 2020, she was notified that her freshman general chemistry course would go virtual. Two days later, even though she and her students were caught off guard, her class of about thirty undergrads met online without a hitch.

Sharma says she taught her online course almost exactly as she did on campus, except that instead of lecturing at the front of her classroom and displaying PowerPoint slides, she now lectures by videoconferencing and shares her digital images with students working on laptops at home.

"Students didn't have to suffer. Their lives were not put on hold," Sharma said of the decision to move courses online. "They seem to have grown up overnight."

WE ARE ALL ONLINE LEARNERS NOW

One thing that made the transition for Sharma and her students easier was that, like nearly all of us, we all participate in online learning informally every day, simply by shopping online, posting on social media, and streaming movies. Whenever we do email or chat with friends on FaceTime, we learn online. So even if faculty and students had never enrolled in or taught an online class before, most were already quite familiar with the virtual experience. We are all online learners now.

Beyond that, two key technologies really made a difference—learning management systems (LMSs) (Ubell, 2019a) and videoconferencing (Kagan, 2019). When the pandemic hit, nearly every U.S. college and university had already installed these two technologies. Without them, schools could never have been up and running online so seamlessly and so quickly.

Most of us by now are very familiar with videoconferencing services like Google Meet, Zoom, and Webex. Even before the pandemic, you may have joined webinars or participated in a videoconference at work. An LMS, on the other hand, is a far more structured platform. Designed especially for teaching and learning, it enables instructors to create course materials, assess student progress, and generate custom exams. With an LMS, students can communicate with their peers and instructors with text, voice, and video; they can also enroll in courses seamlessly, with attendance and grades recorded automatically. Many online courses employ both an LMS and some sort of videoconferencing service.

For those new to virtual teaching, Zoom and its many competitors, are very seductive. Videoconferencing platforms are surprisingly easy to master, and the on-screen, real-time experience replicates a sense of being in a classroom, face-to-face with students. Of course, your students are not actually seated before you; their images are arrayed in rows on your screen as in a stamp album. Instructors can easily adopt exactly the same conventional pedagogical approaches they followed on campus. Given how easy videoconferencing is to grasp, it's unsurprising that its adoption at U.S. colleges leaped ahead of LMS usage during the crisis (Hill, 2020c).

6 Emergency Online Learning

Since the invasion of the coronavirus, a good part of the world shifted to working from home, with Zoom zooming past its videoconferencing rivals. Amazingly, just like Google, Zoom is now a verb. On March 23, 2020, Zoom was downloaded 2.13 million times worldwide. Just two months earlier, merely 56,000 applications were logged on (Kelly, 2020). Today, the company is valued at $140 billion (Macrotrends, 2020).

Earlier, in the fall of 2019, I led a Zoom class at The New School, a liberal-arts college in Manhattan, as part of a four-course online certificate, "Designing Online Learning Programs" (see Chapter 9). One crucial difference between my course and others in the spring 2020 pandemic semester is that my Zoom sessions weren't the entirety of my students' educational experience. Rather, each was the culmination of a week of other academic engagements that included watching brief video lectures I'd recorded earlier, reading excerpts from scholarly articles, and participating in a text-based, peer-to-peer discussion. My hour-long Zoom sessions were real-time discussions, wrapping-up what my students had learned throughout the week. I never delivered a lecture on Zoom.

PANDEMIC PEDAGOGY

Contrast that with pandemic pedagogy. Most faculty had no time to prepare a virtual course that drew thoughtfully on valuable pedagogical methods, like active learning, project-based inquiry, and peer-to-peer instruction. Such methods were championed early in the last century by progressive education giants such as John Dewey, Jean Piaget, and Paulo Freire. The benefits of active learning—whether on screen or on campus—are also supported by recent research in cognitive science and neuroscience (Feldman, 2020).

"What we did [in the spring 2020 semester] is not exactly online learning," admitted Duke University's Shawn Miller, director of Duke Learning Innovation, the school's teaching and learning center, which led Duke's online transition during the spring 2020 crisis. "It's a first-aid approach. In well-designed online courses, faculty have time to prepare, to think about designing a course with prerecorded and other off-line materials. Without planning, faculty just take their face-to-face lectures and put them online."

Compare that with the experience of students enrolled in well-designed digital courses. In numerous studies, most online learners come away with positive feelings. In a classic study, 94 percent said they learned as much or more in their digital course as they did on campus (Fredericksen, 2019).

Heading home in the pandemic didn't provide shelter from the storm for all. Many student homes had no computer or internet access; others, limited bandwidth. While three-quarters of U.S. city inhabitants and 79 percent of suburban residents are plugged into broadband access, just two-thirds of rural Americans are covered. Because the FCC's broadband maps classify a ZIP code as "served," even if merely one home has access, it's impossible to measure how widespread or underserved service actually is (Chin, 2020).

WHAT HAPPENED

Waiting for colleges and universities to reopen, it was anyone's guess as to how many students would actually show up. Some imagined they would stay away out of fear of the continued threat of the disease or out of a desire to stay close to home. With millions out of work, many would be unable to pay tuition (Thompson, 2020). Some predicted crushing student enrollment declines of twenty to thirty percent.

That fall, in a National Student Clearinghouse Research Center count, undergraduate enrollment dropped four percent and community colleges, more than nine percent; while graduate numbers increased by nearly three percent, a jump commonly due to a constricting job market, when those who fail to find work turn to graduate school. But the biggest news was that colleges suffered a shattering loss of nearly 26 percent of first-time college students failing to show up (Hill, 2020c). The results weren't as devastating as pessimists had estimated, but the losses shook higher ed as never before.

As the world economy skittered to the edge, with global consumption collapsing and unemployment surging, higher education was not spared. Colleges and universities were hit hard. Collectively, they stood to lose billions of dollars, with plummeting enrollments, sports events canceled, cafeterias and dorms closed, and nonpandemic research on hold. The University of Michigan, for example, expected a shortfall of $400 million to $1 billion (Fies and Hill, 2020). Some schools, struggling before COVID-19, simply closed their doors for good. In the eight terrible months since the pandemic terrified the country—from March to October 2020—eight U.S. colleges went under. *The New York Times* projected a loss of $23 billion in U.S. higher education revenue from the damage (New York Times, 2020).

According to the U.S. Bureau of Labor Statistics, the coronavirus was responsible for shedding seven percent of the nation's college workforce. An estimated 337,000 fewer workers were employed by private and public colleges in the midst of the pandemic in August 2020, compared with higher ed employment just before COVID hit in February 2020 (Bauman,

8 Emergency Online Learning

2020). Not since the late nineteen-fifties did so many in higher education lose their jobs.

"Never in history has humanity experienced something along this scale and scope," observed Columbia University's Wafaa El-Sadr (Hessler, 2020).

Before the pandemic, more than a third of faculty at U.S. colleges said that online learning isn't as good as face-to-face instruction (Lederman, 2019). No doubt, many of those who taught online in the pandemic still hold that view. In a *Nature* survey, many faculty members in the United States, United Kingdom, and European Union, delivering digital courses in the crisis, reported being unprepared, unsupported, and fearful of the forced culture change. They worried that virtual instruction will result in faculty obsolescence and, ultimately, unemployment (Watermeyer, 2020).

"It's the end of the 'traditional learning space' as we know it," one respondent lamented.

As colleges and universities around the world reopened, millions of instructors and their students reported conflicting reactions to the great experiment in pandemic pedagogy.

"Some faculty may come out of this experience not at all happy. They'll be glad to return to face-to-face teaching when they go back to campus," said Duke's Miller. "Others may be surprised at how good the technology is. The stigma of online learning will be softened a bit."

The astonishing lesson is that online education, so long derided by traditional academics, came to the rescue of conventional higher education.

* * *

By the time you read this, COVID-19 very likely will have passed through its worst phase. Most of the world may have largely returned to a semblance of normality. This is my best hope. But prediction, notoriously, is a very bad business, likely to hit its mark as often as it misses. The wisest move is not to make blind guesses, following Yogi Berra's sage, contradictory advice, "It's tough to make predictions, especially about the future."

That's why, as you read the chapters that follow, you will see that I hesitated to say much about the effects of the pandemic on the future of digital education. As I write, the coronavirus is still keeping many at home, preventing most of us from heading off to work in close quarters at universities as in industry.

But the trembling future has not prevented others from taking stabs at how virtual instruction may fare, once the pandemic is behind us. Unnerved by the crisis, some predict a dystopian future, with elite schools partnering with Silicon Valley venture capitalists, transforming the higher ed economy. Others fear cascading failures of hundreds of colleges (Govindorajan, 2020).

Some observers, however, anticipate fewer threatening consequences, guessing that online learning will shift from a corner of higher ed to its very center, with college leaders finally accepting virtual education as a strategic priority. Some may even reconsider outsourcing digital learning to online program managers (OPMs), favoring building home-grown virtual infrastructure instead (Kim, 2020).

Even so, worried that with depleted resources—owing to alarming declines in tuition and other revenue—schools may not have the capital to launch vital, new online academic programs on their own to take them into more marketable virtual spaces. That's why some schools are hedging their bets already, signing deals to build new digital education degrees with OPM money (Schwartz, 2020) (see Chapter 6).

With nearly all of higher education colleges online during the pandemic, one might claim that digital education had finally triumphed over conventional instruction. In the U.S., it took a quarter of a century to go from zero to enrolling nearly seven million online, but in just about a month, the pandemic spring drove twenty million college students, fleeing from potentially contagious residential classrooms, to safety online (National Center for Education Statistics, 2020).

You might chalk it up as a great accomplishment—if everyone who attended virtual classes did so willingly—but many showed up resentful, taking digital courses only by force of circumstance. Learning online under duress is not exactly the best academic experience, with students enrolled, not because they are eager to participate, but because there was no choice. The alternative was just too dangerous.

As the virus continued to spread over the country as the fall 2020 semester approached, many institutions kept their gates closed. Others remained open under strict social-distancing guidelines and swab testing, but just as quickly—when infections raced through campuses—many retreated, closing before things got out of hand. For many students that harrowing year, you were either online, in hybrid classes, or not in college (Marris, 2020).

Even though online education saved the university earlier that spring, not all those rescued were grateful. For many, there was little to be thankful for, since what they experienced virtually was not exactly top-of-the-line virtual instruction, but catch-as-catch-can improvisation, with most faculty teaching online not knowing exactly what they were doing.

It wasn't very surprising, as college students Zoomed the pandemic away, that few were happy. In a wide-ranging survey of about a thousand students

10   Emergency Online Learning

and instructors, merely eight percent of those online during the crisis say their experience was very effective. An earlier study supported these results, with seven out of ten students studying online in the emergency saying that remote learning was not as good as on-campus instruction, with most finding online classes less engaging (Top Hat, 2020).

Apart from their disappointment in emergency remote learning, largely owing to inadequate instruction, delivered by poorly prepared faculty, students also regretted lack of social interaction online. Universities are not only sites of academic engagement, but equally places where students find lifelong friends, future workplace colleagues, and even lovers. Among the common failures of emergency virtual education was the poverty of social life.

To avoid feelings of alienation online, skilled digital instructors encourage active student participation. Some even claim that online students can come away from a virtual course feeling closer to their online classmates than to their on-campus peers (DeBrock et al., 2020).

I remember as a student long ago at Brooklyn College, sitting next to classmates all semester, nodding hello occasionally, but never once saying a word, departing the course, not even knowing their names.

On campus, what happens in hallways, cafeterias, and dorms is crucial. COVID has not only emptied my neighborhood's movie theaters and local restaurants, but it has also deserted many of the nation's campuses where most of university student life happens.

Many on-campus instructors command in-person lectures like seasoned stage performers, exploiting tension, timing, and humor with dramatic effect. Online, instructor's stand-up routines, honed in years of practice, have little effect, since veteran teachers—as all online faculty now—are mostly hidden from view or seen on-screen in a checkerboard image.

If colleges were to open in that terrible 2020 semester, while the pandemic was still careening across the country, it surely required that classes be held at least partially—or entirely—online, but many institutions squandered the summer, debating whether to open, investigating various safety measures, exploring hybrid or flex options, and sadly, failing to get faculty up to speed in high-quality digital instruction.

Higher education has always privileged research over teaching. For most faculty, pedagogy is for kindergarteners, inappropriate in college. It's no wonder that when remote learning flooded our universities in the pandemic— except for a handful of schools that take college teaching seriously—few senior academic officers recognized that faculty training would be decisive. Instead, they went ahead, plugging into Zoom, trusting that technology alone would do the trick.

We Are All Online Learners Now   11

"By the time we decided to go remote, a third of the summer had gone by," lamented Ilan Jacobsohn, former senior director, distributed education at The New School. "We should have focused on creating excellent virtual teaching examples in high-enrollment courses, as a way of exposing most students to the most positive online learning experience. It was a lost opportunity."

Zoom—and its videoconferencing cousins—was a spectacular success in the crisis, not because it's a perfect online learning tool, but because it tries to replicate the conventional classroom. Colleges adopted it because it closely resembled the on-campus experience. It was a comfortable step to go from physical to virtual space, without reimagining what it might take to teach effectively online. Most faculty just continued Zooming online as they always taught on campus. If hour-long lectures were deadly on campus, they were even deadlier on Zoom.

The impulse—to mimic conventional classrooms online as closely as possible—was followed earlier by MOOCs, massive online learning courses. Only instead of watching real-time instructors delivering lectures in tiny squares on Zoom, MOOC students watched faculty lecturing over streaming videos. The basic flaw in both instances is the conceptual error that the classroom is the ideal place for learning, leading to a parallel mistake, that reproducing it virtually is as close to an authentic educational experience as possible.

In the early days of movies, viewers in theaters watched the screen up front as a black and white curtain seemed to part, replicating the opening of a stage performance. But it didn't take Hollywood very long to realize that moving-picture audiences did not come to see a conventional play, but something new and exciting—a technological marvel, coupled with inventive directorial brilliance—an entirely new mode, not a play at all.

When professors finally recognize that their conventional classroom performances do not quite fit online, they will realize that Zoom, and other digital arts, often act effectively as support services for quality online teaching, not as a substitute. Zoom is quite an inventive piece of digital wizardry, but it is not a replacement for thinking deeply about how students learn. For online learning to be most effective, students must do the principal work of discovery, while faculty, like film directors, stand behind the screen.

A survey of higher ed academic leaders, conducted before the pandemic, revealed that most institutions weren't "prepared to flip a switch and move all their learning into truly online settings." That's why so many colleges embraced Zoom and other video platforms during the crisis, teaching on the fly. Ron Legon of Quality Matters, one of the sponsors of the survey, said

12 Emergency Online Learning

"those who have only a limited understanding of online learning, or have avoided it all together, are likely to be disappointed, frustrated and perhaps confirmed in their belief that this is not a viable alternative to traditional classroom education" (Lederman, 2020).

Online learning in the U.S. is widely acknowledged as by far the most advanced in the world, admired and followed everywhere. Curiously, experts were not always enlisted to lead the transition from in-person to virtual education in the pandemic. To their credit, some schools reached out to experienced teaching and learning centers, such as at Duke, with on-campus units often at the front lines of the transformation to digital learning, guiding the university in making its way through the crisis (Kim and Maloney, 2020). At other institutions, digital learning authorities—many who had been running virtual education programs for years—were not always consulted, with the move online entrusted to others with little or no expertise. Although widely credited with deep respect for knowledge, bafflingly, universities often act no differently from other bureaucracies, carelessly turning to trusted colleagues, rather than the ablest and most competent.

To be fair, as colleges faced their most devastatingly vulnerable crisis in history, confronting steep enrollment declines and financial ruin—and with the health and safety of faculty, staff, and students at terrifying risk—it's no wonder academic leaders fumbled getting instructors up to speed with digital engagement. On campus, pedagogy was never the most pressing objective for the nation's presidents and provosts. Consequently, digital instruction has rarely risen to the top either—even in a pandemic—as the fate of the university was perilously hanging on the threat of the coronavirus.

Teaching online demands that instructors find new ways of captivating students they often can neither see nor hear, a radical departure from centuries of conventional instruction. Virtual instruction does not depend on one's expressive face, spirited movements, or an affecting speaking voice, but on altogether new pedagogies introduced in the last century and practiced by inventive early adopters in this century. To recover from the stumbling emergency semester, surely the first item on the higher ed agenda was to guide faculty in digital instruction best practices.

"COVID's forced shift to remote learning was a once-in-a-century opportunity to re-engineer courses to active learning," declared Ryan Craig in *Inside Higher Ed* (Craig, 2020).

During the pandemic, few college students were exposed to the radical practices championed by digital education. Most emergency instruction—except for online classes taught by veteran digital faculty, who had been teaching virtually long before the crisis—Zoomed ahead with little or no experience, teaching online mostly as they had on campus all along, largely unaware of a quarter of a century of online practice, steering students away from passive video and live Zoom lectures and toward active student participation in project-based, peer-to-peer engagement.

From its very start, early online adopters recognized that talking heads were not right. New pedagogical practices were needed to engage students studying far from campus, most at home, plugging-in remotely after dinner, soon after bedtime stories ended with "happily ever after."

REFERENCES

Bauman, D. (2020, October 6). The Pandemic Has Pushed Hundreds of Thousands of Workers Out of Higher Education. *Chronicle of Higher Education.*

Chin, M. (2020, October 7). America's Internet Wasn't Prepared for Online School. *Verge.*

Craig, R. (2020, September 4). Colleges Should Go Back to School on Remote Learning. *Inside Higher Ed.*

DeBrock, Larry et al. (2020, March 18). The Human Element in Online Learning. *Inside Higher Ed.*

Feldman, R. S. (Ed.). (2020). *Learning Science.* New York: McGraw-Hill.

Fies, Andy and James Hill. (2020, April 28). Coronavirus Pandemic Brings Staggering Losses to Colleges and Universities. *ABC News.*

Fredericksen, Eric. (2019, March). Student Satisfaction and Perceived Learning with Online Courses. *Online Learning.*

Govindorajan, V. (2020, March 31). What the Shift to Virtual Learning Could Mean for the Future of Higher Ed. *Harvard Business Review.*

Hessler, P. (2020, October 5). Nine Days in Wuhan, the Ground Zero of the Coronavirus Pandemic. *The New Yorker.*

Hill, P. (2020a, March 22). U.S. Higher Ed Set to Go Fully Online in Just Four Weeks Due to COVID-19. *Phil on EdTech.*

Hill, P. (2020b, April 2). Massive Increase in LMS and Synchronous Video Usage Due to COVID-19. *Phil on EdTech.*

Hill, P. (2020c, October 15). Quite an Update on Fall 2020 Enrollment in US. *Phil on EdTech.*

Kagan, J. (2019, May 21). Video Conferencing. *Investopia.*

Kelly, S. M. (2020, March 27). Zoom's Massive 'Overnight Success' Actually Took Nine Years. *CNN Business.*

Kim, Joshua. (2020, April 1). Teaching and Learning After COVID-19. *Inside Higher Ed.*

Kim, Joshua and Edward Maloney. (2020). *Learning Innovation and the Future of Higher Education.* Baltimore: Johns Hopkins University Press.

Lederman, D. (2019, October 30). Professors' Slow, Steady Acceptance of Online Learning: A Survey. *Inside Higher Ed.*

Lederman, D. (2020, March 25). The State of Online Education, Before Coronavirus. *Inside Higher Ed.*

14 Emergency Online Learning

Macrotrends. (2020, October 12). Zoom Video Communications Market Cap 2019–2020. *Macrotrends.*

Marris, E. (2020, August 27). The Giant University COVID Experiment. *Nature,* 584.

National Center for Education Statistics. (2020, August 21). *Fast Facts.* Retrieved from https://nces.ed.gov/fastfacts/display.asp?id=372

New York Times. (2020, October 18). By the Numbers Colleges and COVID Stats. *New York Times (Learning).*

Schwartz, N. (2020, October 20). Colleges Look to OPMs as Pandemic Intensifies Shift Online. *Education Dive.*

Thompson, D. (2020, March 20). The Coronavirus Will Be a Catastrophe for the Poor. *The Atlantic.*

Top Hat. (2020, May 1). *Adrift in a Pandemic: Survey of 3,089 Students Finds Uncertainty About Returning to College.* Retrieved from https://tophat.com/press-releases/adrift-in-a-pandemic-survey/

Ubell, R. (2019a, February 20). Online Learning's 'Greatest Hits'. *EdSurge.*

Ubell, R. (2019b, November 6). Higher Ed Has Now Split into Dual Economies: Online and Traditional. *EdSurge.*

Watermeyer, Richard. (2020, April 9). Forced Shift to Online Teaching in Coronavirus Pandemic Unleashes Educators' Deepest Job Fears. *Nature Index.*

Section 2
Theory and Practice

2

Theory and Practice

I must confess the humiliating truth—after more than two decades of cajoling dig-their-heels-in, grumbling faculty to go online—I'd never taught online myself. But now, it was finally my turn.

As head of digital education, my formidable job was to encourage reluctant professors to set aside their qualms, step away from their comfortably proud position at the front of the classroom, and do what many thought was the repellent thing.

For years, I led hundreds of faculty members to the virtual well, gratified that they were responsible for instructing about thirty thousand online learners over my career, but I never got close to teaching on screen. I'd been an online general who sent his virtual troops into battle but, shamefully, never fought in the digital trenches myself. It was time to step up.

In the fall of 2019, Ilan Jacobsohn, former senior director for distributed education at The New School, a small liberal-arts college in Manhattan, asked me to lead a four-course online certificate, "Designing Online Learning Programs," and as part of it, teach a course on online student recruitment. Happily, I enlisted three close colleagues to join me, all noted digital education experts. I wrapped it up with a five-week virtual course, "Finding and Keeping Online Learners" (see Chapter 9).

But I hesitated. It was a terrific opportunity to practice what I preached. When I urged faculty members to teach online, I encouraged them with

18   Theory and Practice

all sorts of positive academic inducements. Virtual classes give students, unable to come to campus—owing to work, family, and other obligations—perhaps their only chance to earn a college degree. Online, I advocated, is the perfect medium to move away from ubiquitous lectures, offering professors a pathway to introduce active-learning pedagogy into the curriculum.

Professors often countered with the discredited belief that online was not as good as face-to-face. They also thought, mistakenly, that it was far more time-consuming than teaching on campus, distracting them from concentrating on research. Still, the biggest justification for resistance was that most were quite happy continuing to lecture face-to-face. Why should they go online when most were entirely gratified doing just what they were doing?

A 2012 *Inside Higher Ed* faculty survey reported that nearly two-thirds of the nation's professors say they believe online learning outcomes are inferior to those in comparable face-to-face courses. Naturally, instructors at schools that deliver virtual programs say they are far more positive about the quality of online learning (Allen and Seaman, 2012), but a more recent *Inside Higher Ed* study reports that, by and large, faculty members continue to question whether online education produces student outcomes equivalent to in-person courses (Inside Higher Ed, 2019).

"Despite their scholarly credentials, a vocal slice of professors and administrators remain skeptical of research into the strength of online programs," concludes former *Chronicle of Higher Education* editor Jeffrey J. Selingo. "This persists even as every new study of online learning arrives at essentially the same conclusion: Students who take all or part of their classes online perform better than those who take the same course through traditional instruction" (Selingo, 2013). Since then, with nearly all U.S. college professors teaching online in the 2020 pandemic, faculty opinion about digital education has been on a rollercoaster ride (see Chapter 1).

A Tyton Partners survey, conducted in the middle of the virus, uncovered a surprising shift, with nearly half of college faculty saying that online learning is an effective teaching method, a dramatic departure from the widely acknowledged, more negative previous faculty opinion. It's a fascinating result, since most faculty who participated in emergency digital instruction did not find pandemic virtual education very good (Top Hat, 2020). The new, counterintuitive finding may have emerged from the fact that most professors had little experience with remote instruction before the crisis; merely having hands-on familiarity with it could have made the difference.

Earlier, a comprehensive literature survey by Steven A. Lloyd, Michelle M. Byrne, and Tami S. McCoy confirmed that most faculty believed that digital education is not nearly as effective as classroom instruction because online teachers do not exchange visual cues with students (Lloyd, 2012).

The term "face-to-face" implies a fairly close relationship between student and instructor, with the teacher up front in an intimate classroom setting with students seated in close proximity. One does not commonly refer to actors performing on a theater stage or athletes in a giant stadium as being face-to-face with their audience. In most colleges, students—commonly freshmen, but others as well, even as they rise through academic life—are often seated in mammoth lecture halls in which the relationship between professor and student is more like performer and spectator, with faculty members at lecterns facing seas of faces. At the University of Colorado, for example, 33 courses seat four hundred or more students, with three classes shockingly occupied by more than 1,200. One chemistry course is so big that the final exam is given in the school's basketball arena (Associated Press, 2013).

"For students who sit in the back rows of an auditorium, every large face-to-face lecture class is a distance ed course," mocks Steven Mintz of the University of Texas at Austin (Mintz, 2020).

Of course, seminars for upper-division students are not nearly as packed and can be stirring academic experiences, with faculty and students thoughtfully absorbed in engaging dialog. And we are often mesmerized by thrilling lectures delivered by penetrating scholars, even in big spaces, as I was as an undergraduate at Brooklyn College in an enthralling Shakespeare class in a large assembly hall. But as we all know from our own college days, not every professor is equally compelling. Often, students are sedated by less than electrifying scholastic performances, especially in huge academic auditoriums, with students secretly texting their friends under their desks.

Years ago, I audited a cell biology class at Columbia University, where hundreds of us were stacked in long rows in a vast indoor amphitheater as PowerPoint slides whizzed by. It was not an especially illuminating way to learn about cell function and structure.

In the nineteen-fifties, social scientist Erving Goffman, who studied face-to-face interactions, questioned faculty confidence in their ability to know how attentive students are. Goffman recognized that people can display false attention so that they appear alert.

"We have party faces, funeral faces, and various kinds of institutional faces," (Goffman, 1963). Goffman recognized that while people may appear

20 Theory and Practice

engaged, they often can hide behind what he called "involvement shields," busy with side activities, like doodling or texting.

While instructors commonly believe that student engagement is easily observed, reading learner participation is not always obvious, especially in large lecture halls. With smiles, nods, and other signs, students can disguise boredom, hostility, frustration, and other feelings that may camouflage that they are not paying close attention.

"In class, eagerness, attention, and alertness are often taken as signs that students are all ears," I acknowledged (Ubell, 2016). "But Goffman says that these behaviors are often merely performances, encouraged by academic culture to elicit certain approved responses, leading students to achieve faculty and peer acceptance by exhibiting disciplined conformity."

The largely unquestioned confidence in the superiority of face-to-face instruction is supported neither by student experience nor scholarly evidence. Indeed, a massive—now classic—U.S. Department of Education meta-analysis of the literature showed that students taking online classes performed modestly better than their peers studying on campus, with those in blended courses performing better than both (Means et al., 2010). Since then, hundreds of articles confirm that, on the whole, student results are almost indistinguishable, with student learning in blended classes consistently superior.

Still, not every review of the scholarly literature is as enthusiastic about the success of online learning. A recent study by Ithaka S+R, a nonprofit research and consulting group, casts some doubt on the rigor of research methods employed by the big Department of Education meta-analysis, noting that some researchers are unhappy with the evidence, pointing to later studies that undermine some online results (Lack, 2013). Ithaka's review concluded that there is a lack of serious efficacy studies comparing online with in-person education, calling for a national effort comparable to randomized controlled clinical drug trials.

The widespread perception that in-person education is best persists despite continuing deep failures in U.S. higher education—unsupportable student debt, discouraging completion rates, and stubborn economic and racial inequalities. The unquestioned support of on-campus learning ignores the results of impressive studies challenging the comfortable assumption that American college teaching is in good hands. In their widely reported study, Richard Arum and Josipa Roksa uncovered the disturbing fact that "a pattern of limited learning is prevalent on contemporary college campuses." They concluded that "a large proposition of gains [by U.S. college students] in critical thinking, complex reasoning and written communication are either exceedingly small or empirically nonexistent" (Arum, 2011).

Many idealize their halcyon schoolroom days, misty with childhood or dreamy with college escapades, illuminated with doubtful memories—nostalgia for times that may have existed mainly in fiction. Most may have forgotten old anxieties, not feeling smart enough, not studying hard enough, sluggish in overheated classrooms as a mumbled lecture in a foreign accent goes on too long, uneasily responding, slumped and mystified, wondering how other classmates seem to get it by nodding and taking notes.

One obstacle I'd never considered is faculty anxiety, especially feelings of technical inadequacy. Even though I've led high-tech academic units for years, I've never been a whiz at digital devices and their puzzling applications. After dinner each night at home, for example, my wife and I sit elbow-to-elbow in armchairs facing our tv. Since I never got the hang of clicking from icon to icon, navigating from Netflix to Hulu to get to our favorite shows for binge-watching, my wife drives. At my office, too, I'm not all that swift when I perform more than the simplest tasks on my computer.

One study of faculty attitudes towards online learning revealed that anxiety about teaching online colored their perceptions. Those who expressed fear of virtual instruction mostly concluded that online learning was inferior to face-to-face teaching (Bunk, 2015).

INSTRUCTIONAL DESIGN

Since digital education first emerged, following the heady early days of the World Wide Web in the nineties, online learning has faced the elusive hurdle of turning disembodied classmates and instructors into living, breathing engaged learners and teachers, with minds and hearts you can feel, know and understand; with whom you can imagine sitting together over a cappuccino in a local café.

Clever techies have stepped up to the challenge with ingenious gadgets, transforming remote students into tangible beings with a heartbeat, devising uncanny innovations, most now surprisingly part of mainstream education right on campus. Zoom, and its video-conference relatives, now give us postage-stamp images on our screens, turning the featureless digital experience into a chorus of faces.

More than two decades ago when I entered the world of online learning, few tools were available to help faculty migrate their on-campus courses online. I'd send instructors off into virtual classrooms, practically on their own, with little or no support. Sink or swim. Courageously, pioneering

22 Theory and Practice

faculty would just dive in, largely unaided by high-tech devices, making do, often in inspired ways, simply and creatively with their wits and ingenuity.

Today, instructional designers, supported by clever, new technologies, are the first responders to animating digital courses. In my previous book, *Going Online*, I recognized that on-campus faculty members are largely on their own. They walk into class with little or no support from either their colleagues or institution, preparing and delivering lectures autonomously (Ubell, 2016). Lone academic wolves. In contrast, virtual instructors are part of a team, collaborating closely with instructional designers, program managers, videographers, and others who help produce technically sophisticated and pedagogically engaging courses.

While I was prepared to teach in an entirely new way—as I had advocated for years—it turned out that New School digital training staff ingeniously guided me in developing my course through the lens of active learning, an approach I had long championed. My instructional designer, Shira Richman, assistant director of distributed learning at the time, guided me through it all like a coach training an athlete for a big game, unknotting my fears and unraveling my anxieties.

Best of all, Shira built my confidence week after week. On Wednesday afternoons over several months, in one of New York City's most glamorous, Hollywood-style landmarks, designed by the avant-garde architect Joseph Urban, Shira and I met for an hour each week in a back office, away from imagined smirks and snickers at my amateur skills. As weeks passed, she held my novice hand as we navigated together through what for me was totally unchartered territory.

As you'd expect, while professors are experts in their fields, most have little experience teaching online. Faculty, trained in their disciplines, are rarely prepared to teach, even in face-to-face classes. Doctoral candidates focus almost entirely on research and receive little or no formal practice teaching. "Graduate students are not only entering classrooms without much preparation," observed Richard Arum, dean of the University of California, Irvine School of Education, "but more problematically, they are learning in their graduate programs to deprioritize and perhaps even devalue teaching" (Arum, 2011).

Faced with increasingly complex communication technologies—voice, video, multimedia, gaming, animation—university faculty, expert in their own disciplines, find themselves technically perplexed, largely unprepared to build digital courses. Online places a burden on faculty they had not foreseen when they signed up for academic life. After all, most professors started out believing they were destined to do scholarly work, perform research, publish results, and teach in classrooms. For most, teaching online was not what they had in mind.

As sophisticated digital skills—capabilities ironically found more commonly among students—became decisive, two new trends emerged. The bigger one occurred when instructional designers, long employed by industry, joined online academic teams, working closely with faculty to upload and integrate interactive and engaging content. Well-trained instructional designers marshal a deep reservoir of methods. They help faculty design virtual courses that encourage peer-to-peer interaction, devising targeted questions, group discussions, and virtual teaming. Instructional designers work with faculty to open online courses to prompting during an activity and feedback after assignments are submitted. They recommend frequent quick quizzes and other ways of demonstrating knowledge, such as group work, demonstrations, portfolios, and presentations.

The next big move in the evolution of digital education came when instructional designers, as part of their skillset, turned to digital authoring systems, software introduced to stimulate engagement, encouraging virtual students to interface actively with digital materials, often by tapping at a keyboard or touching the screen as in a video game. Most authoring software also integrates assessment tools, testing learning outcomes.

With authoring software, instructional designers, together with faculty, can steer online students through a mixtape of digital content—videos, graphs, weblinks, PDFs, drag-and-drop activities, PowerPoint slides, quizzes, survey tools, and so on. Some systems also offer video editing, recording, and screen downloading options.

"The good news is that you don't need to be a programmer to build high-production-value online courses," said John Vivolo, director of online education at the Katz School of Yeshiva University, and a former NYU colleague. "All you need is your imagination."

The digital transformation of higher education will be led in part by instructional designers, skilled at knowing how to put a course together—online or on campus—to maximize each student's ability to learn. Astute instructional designers base their pedagogical methods on learning science, a new multidiscipline domain, that has formulated a set of key elements drawn from recent intensive research on how people learn (National Research Council, 2000).

Widely adopted course design principles, following many basic practices in online education, can be found at Quality Matters (Quality Matters, 2020) and the Online Learning Consortium Quality Scorecard (OLC Quality Scorecard, 2020). Institutions adopt these rubrics as field guides for

24 Theory and Practice

building and assessing online courses. Most can be implemented equally on campus and online. They are practical roadmaps for faculty, students, instructional designers, and others who play roles in introducing digital education in colleges and universities. Some institutions use them as checklists for faculty and instructional designers to make sure they cross all the t's and dot all the i's before mounting courses on each school's digital learning platform.

Others follow ADDIE—Analysis, Design, Development, Implementation, and Evaluation—a framework for creating instructional materials. New approaches are often ADDIE spinoffs, with rapid prototyping a commonly accepted improvement, exploiting continuous feedback as new items are introduced online (Chappell, 2018).

Shira, my instructional designer, was especially clever about guiding me on how I might eventually deliver my recorded lectures, planned to run no more than seven minutes each, a widely recognized limit, acknowledging that brief videos are best in maintaining student focus—a wise alternative to long-winded lectures. Shira shadowed me with probing questions, helping me tease out what would emerge as my most effective delivery.

As I jabbered randomly, exploring how best to organize my thoughts, Shira tapped away at her keyboard. Magically, she transformed my inchoate utterances into compact, arrow-sharp bullet points. Like a hypnotist, she rummaged through my mind to extract my most salient thoughts.

As we continued laying out what each week would cover—market research, websites, digital recruitment, and so on—Shira and I tossed ideas back and forth, suggesting active-learning challenges I would pitch to remote students. Which ones would be reserved for synchronous delivery and which would I offer asynchronously? Following my taped lecture on student retention, Shira and I thought it best to open the class to synchronous discussion.

In line with active-learning theory, I proposed that in each of the five weeks my course ran, I'd open an hourlong, real-time discussion session to allow participants to ask questions about the week's topic or engage in peer-to-peer discussion, giving students the chance to explore with one another what they had discovered from open-source documents, research reports, and readings I'd recommended. It's a similar pedagogical style practiced in so-called "flipped" classrooms, in which learners on their own read the literature, digging into online and conventional sources, and then show up in class on campus to engage in open discussions with their instructor and their classmates (see Chapter 13). "The basic concept is not new, of course," comments Jeffrey J. Selingo in *College Unbound*. "Literature classes have been taught this way for decades. Read the book outside of class and discuss its characters and themes in class" (Selingo, 2013).

Now, at last, I was turning theory into practice—actually doing what I had only imagined. In one of Yogi Berra's inimitable, but surprisingly insightful, contradictions, "In theory there is no difference between theory and practice. In practice there is."

One day, as we came close to filling in the last color on my planning charts, showing completed drafts of my lectures, active-learning challenges, resources, slides, readings, and syllabi for each week, Ilan Jacobsohn, the head of online learning at The New School, wondered whether I was all set for my first recording sessions.

"I'm not at ease," I acknowledged. "I worry about my confidence. When I listen to tapes of webinars I've delivered, I often cringe hearing my hesitations and repeated 'uh-uh,' put-putting like a failing car engine."

Ilan listened closely. "Everyone is worried about how they will perform. Most faculty are not trained, but you'll be in a very supportive environment during your video sessions," Ilan reassured me. "Just a few students in the studio."

"Between takes," he continued, "students usually carry on lively conversations with the faculty. They are very interested in what instructors are saying. It's very intimate. Quite relaxing."

Ilan relieved my worries by saying that if the first recordings are not up to standard, they do get progressively more polished. "Occasionally," he predicted, "at the end of a session, if your first videos are not at their best, and if there's still time, the crew goes back to re-record them."

CONSTRUCTIVISM

In grade school, I remember sitting at my desk at P.S. 135 in Brooklyn, lips sealed, hands clasped in front of me on a wooden desktop, carved with a long, slender channel for pencils and pens, with a dark, empty inkwell, splattered with black stains, inserted inches away at the far right.

The radical Brazilian pedagogical philosopher, Paulo Freire, following other exasperated education theorists—John Dewey, Lev Vygotsky, and Jerome Bruner, among others—scorned the conventional classroom, making fun of my favorite teacher, Mrs. Rosenberg, for depositing knowledge in my mind as if it were a piggy bank.

Freire ridiculed the "empty mind, passively open to the reception of deposits of reality from the world outside." According to Freire, the "banking concept" interferes with intellectual growth by turning students into silent

26 Theory and Practice

receptors, collectors of information, rather than engaged in active participation, building knowledge together with others (Freire, 1971).

Little has changed since Victorian times in colleges and universities in the U.S. today—except, of course, students now come to class in t-shirts and distressed jeans, never embarrassed by the social *faux pas* of neat jackets and blouses. But knowledge deposits into minds are still the most common way of teaching, even after the invasion of decades of teaching technologies and despite strong evidence that traditional lectures are not nearly as effective as active learning.

According to *The Chronicle of Higher Education*, the "Lecture remains the dominant or exclusive mode of teaching in many college classrooms today" (Lang, 2006). Stanford Nobel laureate Carl Wieman and Harvard's Eric Mazur have compared the lecture to watching a marathon on tv to learn how to run (Gross-Loh, 2016).

A recent study in the *Proceedings of the National Academy of Sciences* found that undergraduate students in classes taught by traditional lectures are 1.5 times more likely to fail than students whose faculty deliver active learning instruction (Freeman et al., 2014). The paper analyzed 225 studies in a meta-analysis of undergraduate STEM teaching methods, concluding that instruction that encouraged students to participate actively, rather than as passive knowledge banks, boosted exam scores and reduced failure rates markedly.

Over a couple of decades, I championed active learning, encouraging online faculty to move away from delivering videotaped lectures only, moving to a broader array of real-time and asynchronous on-screen and keyboard activities including peer-to-peer learning, virtual teamwork, and digital gaming, among other ways of stimulating remote students to dig into what they are learning, not just passively accept instruction, like spectators at a sports arena.

Frustrated by conventional lessons—often delivered in soporific lectures—early online adopters dreamed that one day their constructivist approach of student-led discovery, would infiltrate residential classes, too.

Constructivism is the idea that people give meaning to the world—rather than that meaning resides in it. Constructivists believe that we forge meaning in our minds as we interact with people and things, experience social phenomena circling around us, absorb thoughts of others, and even examine our own reflections. We make sense of it all by building on our own experiences, collecting and organizing our perceptions and thoughts. Constructivist theory holds that learning occurs in our minds as we adjust to our continuously growing and changing stores of knowledge (Joosten, 2020).

Theory and Practice 27

From its start, constructivism opposed behaviorism, a learning theory championed by B.F. Skinner and others. Behaviorism occupied the dominant paradigm for most of the last century and is still thought central by many. Behaviorism claims that only objectively observable data count in learning, with human beings often treated as though we are machines or biological organisms. Behaviorism holds that people are controlled by their environment and respond to external conditions to which they are subjected (Joosten, 2020).

For constructivists, learning is an active process, with knowledge derived and integrated into our minds as we listen to a lecture delivered in a classroom on campus or online, read a textbook, or uncover knowledge just by being in the world. According to Seymour Papert, a pioneering learning constructivist and founding member of the MIT Media Lab—echoing John Dewey, the American pragmatist philosopher—learning rests on our experience, no matter how or where it occurs (Papert, 1993).

The idea of social constructivism has emerged as central to digital instruction, since it recognizes the significance of knowledge gained through social interaction, drawn principally from the work of Lev Vygotsky, whose work was long suppressed in the Soviet Union, but rediscovered by psychologists in the West in the 1960s (Vygotsky, 1978).

Online instruction at its best, following Vygotsky's insights, acknowledges that productive learning occurs when we interact with one another, exploiting opportunities to learn from each other in a style now known as "peer-to-peer learning" and practiced in virtual teams. When learners engage in common, mutually dependent tasks, they create new or expanded knowledge.

Active learning, also following constructivist practice, has emerged as highly effective, not only online, but on campus, too. In active learning, instructors withdraw from the center of the virtual or residential classroom, giving students the social space and technical tools to build knowledge on their own.

The online experience accommodates itself far more comfortably to active, peer-to-peer learning than the conventional classroom in which students are installed at mostly fixed desks in parallel rows—like observers, rather than participants. Freed from rigid order and the time constraints of the college credit-hour, online students can communicate with each other at will, whenever the opportunity arises—wherever and whenever a flame of insight is ignited, before bed, over lunch, on the subway—to reach out across space and time to engage with their virtual classmates. In online learning, you don't need to raise your hand for permission to explore a new

28   Theory and Practice

thought, to inquire about what others think, or to brainstorm a concept or a proposed solution to a problem. You just go online and spill what's on your mind.

"Digital learning breaks through the constrains of space and time imposed by the physical classroom," I wrote in *Going Online*. "Online, you can explore insights for as long as it takes—an hour, a day, a week—conducting courses in *unbounded time*" (Ubell, 2016).

At their best, online faculty achieve what is known as "teaching presence," a constellation of actions that give students a vivid sense that virtual instructors are fully engaged. Teaching presence emerges from online faculty-student interaction and feedback that exploits email, chat, discussion boards, webinars, and other applications that defy the limits of space and time (Swan, 2004).

Since the introduction of digital education over the past quarter century, we can map teachers' roles as they moved from the center of the educational stage as principal actors in traditional classrooms to the wings in virtual learning. Online, instructors play an entirely new and radical part, setting the stage for students to act on their own. Online faculty now sit in the audience as observers and critics, with students poised as performers, where learning takes place collaboratively with their peers.

Unlike the time constraints imposed by the physical classroom, online instructors and students enter a borderless space, open to the possibility of continuous dialog. In asynchronous communication, the give and take of online discussion is conducted at a much slower pace, giving students and teachers time to reflect and more room for analysis, critique, and problem-solving.

"eLearning leaders need to know that engaged and competent instructors are a critical resource in successful online courses and programs," encourage online scholars Karen Swan of the University of Illinois and Peter Shea of the University at Albany. "They need to be respected and supported, not merely for their teaching presence but also for the social roles they play in eLearning process" (Swan and Shea, 2020).

The night before my first lecture, I awoke at 2:30 a.m. from a nightmare, unable to return to sleep. I slipped out of bed, careful not to disturb my wife, burrowed in a duvet, and took off to the living room sofa, awake until 4:00 a.m. Consciously, it was not the video session the next morning that kept me awake, but the bubbling dailiness of my life. Doubtless, I was suppressing my anxiety over my first-ever video lecture.

The next day, I arrived as directed at 9:00 a.m. at a very professional-looking studio, equipped with giant stage lights and video cameras resting on tripods like tall, steel insects. A long, paper-covered table at the side displayed breakfast goodies—bagels, cream cheese, sliced meats, and cheeses. Coffee was served in large cardboard dispensers, supplied by Murray's, a local Greenwich Village institution nearby. It felt thrilling, as if I had wandered into a sophisticated film shoot. Red Dot, the school's video production staff, consists almost entirely of students, going about their various tasks like Hollywood crew.

As I sat in front of the cameras, as if I were a newscaster on tv, I thought of the weeks that Shira, my instructional designer, and I had devoted to this moment. At first, it all seemed so fragmented, but as the bullet points scrolled up on a screen in front of me, suddenly, it all came together, finally making sense.

Filming at first was bumpy as I stumbled over words and phrases, struggling to deliver the points I hoped to make. The crew was very patient.

"You're doing fine," they encouraged, running another take. As we progressed, and as Ilan had predicted, I felt more comfortable, delivering a string of sentences without stumbling. At the end, as I unbuttoned the top of my shirt to unhook my microphone, I felt I'd done reasonably well.

Later that day, viewing some of the clips from the session in his office, Ilan, the head of The New School's online learning unit, called excitedly.

"You were fantastic!" he exclaimed.

Afterward, I reflected on just how remarkable and unexpected my experience turned out to be. All the preparatory work Shira and I did earlier was surprisingly transformed from random notes, jottings, and bullet points—accompanied by serious jitters—into a sustained and logical script. Later, the crew edited it, adding my slides and marginal text, and merged it all into a five-week online course.

As the course unfolded, students not only viewed my video lectures, but also watched interviews I had conducted with experts on specific topics covered—digital marketing, website creation, and social media, among other themes. In the final session, students delivered their individual projects, based not only on the videos they had watched earlier, but also on books, websites, and articles I had assigned and research they conducted independently.

Each week, students built their final presentations, submitting drafts for preliminary peer-to-peer, offline discussion. In week 5, they wrapped it all up with a slide show, with students presenting what they had uncovered and what they concluded in a real-time webinar, delivered to the rest of the class on Zoom for open discussion and review, as if they were participating in an architecture school "crit," exposing what they had achieved to me and to their peers.

30 Theory and Practice

"Migrating a course from lecture to active learning format is as much work as developing a brand-new course," notes Ryan Craig in *Wired* (Craig, 2018). Most of us might conclude that online education merely requires that faculty faithfully replicate their courses delivered in physical to digital space. It turns out, however, that online learning is not simply the result of introducing technical means to match the campus experience online. Going online is like moving to a foreign country, where you must learn a new language and assimilate a new culture.

REFERENCES

Allen, E. and J. Seaman. (2012). *Conflicted: Faculty and Online Education, 2012.* Washington, DC: Inside Higher Ed.

Arum, R. (2011). *Academically Adrift.* Chicago: University of Chicago Press.

Associated Press. (2013). Monster Class Size Unavoidable at Colleges. *NBC News.*

Bunk, J. (2015, September). Understanding Faculty Attitudes About Distance Education: The Importance of Fear and Excitement. *Online Learning*, 19(4).

Chappell, M. (2018, September 26). Instructional Design Using the ADDIE Model. *eLearnig Industry.* Retrieved from https://elearningindustry.com/addie-model-instructional-design

Craig, R. (2018). Rethinking the Lecture: In the Information Age It's Time to Flip the Classroom. *Wired.*

Freeman, S. et al. (2014, June 10). Active Learning Increases Student Performance in Science, Engineering, and Mathematics. *Proceedings of the National Academy of Sciences*, 111.

Freire, P. (1971). *Pedagogy of the Oppressed.* New York: Herder and Herder.

Goffman, E. (1963). *Behavior in Public Places.* New York: The Free Press.

Gross-Loh, C. (2016, July 14). Should Colleges Really Eliminate the College Lecture? *The Atlantic.*

Inside Higher Ed. (2019). *2019 Survey of Online Attitudes on Technology.* Washington, DC: Inside Higher Ed.

Joosten, T. (2020). Learning Science Research Through a Social Science Lens. In Robert S. Feldman (Ed.), *Learning Science: Theory, Research & Practice.* New York: McGraw-Hill.

Lack, K. A. (2013). *Current Status of Research on Online Learning in Post-Secondary Education.* New York: Ithaka S+R.

Lang, J. M. (2006, September 29). Beyond Lecturing. *Chronicle of Higher Education.*

Lloyd, S. (2012, March). Faculty-Perceived Barriers of Online Education. *MEROLT Journal of Online Learning and Teaching*, 8(1).

Means, B. et al. (2010). *Evaluation of Evidence-based Practices in Online Learning: A Meta-Analysis and Review of Online Learning Studies.* Washington, DC: U.S. Department of Education.

Mintz, S. (2020, October 13). Remote Learning Isn't Going Away. *Inside Higher Ed.*

National Research Council. (2000). *How People Learn: Brain, Mind, Experience, and School* (John D. Bransford, Ed., expanded edition). Washington, DC: National Academy Press.

OLC Quality Scorecard. (2020). Retrieved from https://onlinelearningconsortium.org/consult/olc-quality-scorecard-suite/

Papert, S. (1993). *Mindstorms: Children, Computers and Powerful Ideas*. New York: Basic Books.

Quality Matters. (2020). Retrieved from www.qualitymatters.org/

Selingo, J. (2013). *College Unbound*. New York: Houghton Mifflin Harcourt.

Swan, K. (2004). Learning Online: A Review of Current Research on Issues of Interface, Teaching Presence and Learner Characteristics. In *Elements of Quality in Online Education*. Needham, MA: Sloan Consortium.

Swan, K. and P. Shea. (2020). What eLearning Leaders Should Know About Online Teaching. In G. E. Ives (Ed.), *Leading the eLearning Transformation of Higher Education* (2nd edition). Sterling, VA: Stylus.

Top Hat. (2020, May 1). *Adrift in a Pandemic: Survey of 3,089 Students Finds Uncertainty About Returning to College*. Retrieved from https://tophat.com/blog/adrift-in-a-pandemic-survey-infographic/

Ubell, R. (2016). *Going Online*. New York: Routledge.

Vygotsky, L. (1978). *Mind in Society*. Cambridge, MA: Harvard University Press.

3

Online as an Ethical Practice

From the start, access has been the defining achievement of online learning. Or so I thought.

For a couple of decades, I championed online learning for its ability to uproot entrenched ideas in education, especially by engaging students in active learning, a pedagogical style rarely practiced on campus. But I was even more taken with digital learning's ability to let underrepresented students leap virtually over high campus gates to earn college degrees as never before.

Then came several new studies concluding that low-income students at U.S. community colleges may not be as well served online as their residential peers. One headline in *The New York Times* (Dynarski, 2018) summed-up the findings: "Online Courses Are Harming the Students Who Need the Most Help."

Reading initial coverage of the research, I worried that virtual access may not be accomplishing all that it promised. Is online the educational and economic game changer I thought it was?

So, I took a closer look at a handful of recent studies measuring online against face-to-face at U.S. community colleges. While some showed relatively poor online results, others were not that bad. As has been common since the very first large-scale studies were reported more than ten years ago, blended models—ones that mix and match face-to-face with online— emerged with the strongest outcomes (Means, 2010).

32

Community colleges in the U.S. serve about 5.5 million students (Duffin, 2020), representing about a third of the nation's college population. Students enrolled in two-year, as compared with four-year schools, look very different, with about sixty percent in community colleges drawn from the bottom two rungs of the most economically disadvantaged families, while most students at four-year colleges are from the country's most financially secure ones (Fain, 2019)—a widely acknowledged disparity.

If you want to learn whether online is good for the nation's underserved populations, studying the effects of virtual instruction at community colleges is a good place to start. After all, chances are students taking these courses are not as well-prepared for college as residential students at four-year colleges, and they are commonly drawn from the most economically challenged populations.

A recent Columbia University Teachers College study at the Washington State Community and Technical Colleges (Jaggars, 2011) found that students were more likely to fail or withdraw from online courses than from face-to-face classes. The report also showed that in other outcomes, too, online students were not as strong as their residential peers. In contrast—and as was found in many studies—students were equally likely to complete a hybrid course, one that delivers both face-to-face and digital components, as to complete a face-to-face course.

"Students are more likely to graduate if they blend," remarked Peter Shea, associate provost for online learning at the University of Albany. Shea is also editor-in-chief of the scholarly journal, *Online Learning*.

Another report by the same Columbia team (Xu, 2010), measuring the Virginia Community College System, uncovered similar results—that students were more likely to fail or withdraw from online courses than from face-to-face classes and were less likely in other ways to do as well as in-person learners.

Just as I was most discouraged, I did find some research with a much brighter outlook. Arizona State University concluded that among those who took an online or blended course, retention rates at Houston Community College for first-time freshman were nine to ten percentage points greater than among on-campus students (Belkin, 2018).

Checking to see if the Columbia University team's poor online results at community colleges stood up to large-scale national data, Peter Shea and his colleague, Temi Bidjerano, pulled up data on U.S. student first-year completion rates and found, contrary to the Columbia studies, that students who take some of their early courses online "have a significantly better chance of attaining a community college credential than do their classroom-only counterparts (Shea and Bidjerano, 2014)." I heaved a relieved sigh.

34   Theory and Practice

Karen Swan, James J. Stukel distinguished professor of educational leadership at the University of Illinois, says that her research predicts a few essential features about the composition of online students—apart from being more likely to be female, they are also older and poorer than their face-to-face peers, and consequently, more likely to go online part-time. As expected, part-time students on campus, too, have a high dropout rate. But insightfully, her research concludes that "there is no difference between online and on-campus part-time students" (Swan, 2019).

Virtual education is not a panacea. At Wall Street-backed for-profits and, sadly, even at some exemplary nonprofit institutions too, virtual students are merely fresh fish, ready to be reeled-in for profitable revenue streams. Tossed about in life, underrepresented students are often knocked about again online, with endless video lectures with little or no interaction—no better online than in lecture halls on campus—sending listless students fleeing. Chances are that dispiriting low retention and graduation rates at some schools result from remote students escaping death by PowerPoint.

Digging through the dizzying literature, some observers, focusing on poor outcomes, caution low-income students about going online, fearing that the virtual classroom is a setup, driving them to fail or drop out, causing them to stumble out of higher education without a prized degree in hand.

But the advice given to nontraditional students to stay away from digital education is gratuitous, since low-income, working adults are pretty much stuck. If they're looking to earn a degree, they don't have much choice. Forced to work, they often can't cavalierly quit their jobs and take conventional courses on campus. With families to care for and demands at work, online is surely their best—and may be their only—possible option.

As the economic gap between rich and poor widens, the historic role higher education has played in bridging the divide is more important now than ever (Piketty, 2017).

That's why online education is an ethical practice, especially for those who find it nearly impossible to attend on campus. Online rescues them, giving them the unprecedented opportunity to earn a degree without the stress of commuting or taking classes at night. Since its invention over two decades ago, online has permitted millions of working students to leap over the class divide.

SUPPORTING ONLINE STUDENTS

But instead of entering confidently through the front gate as residential students do, online learners often struggle to scale high college walls virtually.

Online as an Ethical Practice   35

Commonly, once digital students are admitted, schools don't welcome them with the same generosity they offer the conventional, residential population.

As I stepped back and wondered what to conclude, I realized that it's worth focusing on one piece of the puzzle that can be overlooked—student services.

Student services—study centers, career services, healthcare, clubs and support for learning and students with disabilities, among dozens of other benefits—are widely available on many campuses. But few colleges offer the same expansive attention to remote learners. On campus, students are coddled with high-end services, with twenty percent of higher education budgets going to student services and related costs at state schools and thirty percent at private colleges (National Center for Education Statistics, 2019).

In contrast, virtual student support is often an afterthought. In a literature search I performed while researching this chapter, I found just a handful of references covering online services, with none quoting how much schools spend on them—a sign that very little attention is paid and, distressingly, little is invested.

Some colleges hardly consider online services, especially colleges and universities just beginning to think of launching digital programs. Instructional design, technology, and faculty participation are investments that must be made, but my own experience bears out that online student services often don't make the cut. In several programs with which I am familiar, online student services didn't even make it onto the planning agenda. In one case, when it was finally identified as something that should be addressed, it took months for a special committee to be formed. Regrettably, it met only once and, alarmingly, no action was ever taken.

When budget records are silent, it's a sure sign that very little is actually spent. Most schools hardly give it a thought. It's as if online students don't need anything but digital classrooms taught by virtual instructors to make it through. Most schools act as if remote learners can get along almost entirely on their own, like teenagers playing video games.

While remote learners commonly receive fewer services than their residential peers, surely, they require more. At their best, online staff hover like helicopter parents, inquiring routinely about what's happening in their academic and home lives—wondering, for example, why they didn't post this week on their class forum, why they didn't log in to take their virtual proctored exam, or why they hadn't enrolled in courses for next semester—inquiries that monitor behavior that is crucial in the long run. Commonly, faculty track academic achievement, but student services help remote students get through their stressful daily lives.

36   Theory and Practice

While digital courses give online students access when work and family prevent them from coming to campus, online students confront yet other obstacles—virtual alienation and technical demands for which many are unprepared.

It turns out there are things community colleges as well as the rest of higher education can do, in addition to providing enhanced digital support for remote students. Online learners deserve better—and certainly no less than their richer on-campus peers.

Lisa Bellantuono, now director of graduate admissions operations at George Washington University, who recently ran online student recruitment at the NYU Tandon School of Engineering, is among the most astute leaders recognizing the obstacles virtual students must jump. I worked closely with her at NYU. Long ago, Bellantuono championed life-cycle recruitment and retention, with responsive staff supporting remote learners right from the start, from admissions all the way through to graduation.

Bellantuono stresses the importance of hosting virtual learner orientation sessions, guiding online students on how best to navigate the often-baffling system. "Be truthful about what they are getting into," she emphasized. Skilled staff must run students through what to others may seem trivial—explaining how to submit an assignment or how to communicate effectively with peers in different time zones who may be located practically anywhere in the U.S. or abroad.

The biggest challenge, Bellantuono recognized, is encouraging online students to burrow remotely into campus services, to become embedded in the university, to feel part of it all. Luckily, some on-campus services are available remotely, but not all departments recognize that the university is also home to students at a distance. "Just stop by" is not very helpful to learners in Shanghai.

That's why a few years ago, Arizona State University launched a mobile app, an online one-stop shop, helping students maneuver services, decisively providing robust student engagement. With just one click, students can access the school's academic calendar, library, or any one of dozens of other sites. They can even click on entertainment options available right on the app. Troubled students can even call ASU's Counseling Services to speak directly to a counselor—without an appointment. Convenience and compassion on a mobile phone.

Online units must also be aware that remote students often face financial stress, especially when changing jobs, commonly losing employer sponsorship. "It's tricky to figure out how to collaborate with your school's financial aid office, seeking university aid possibilities for virtual students,"

Bellantuono said. "Financial resources are often readily available for residential students, but rarely for those online."

Apart from accessibility and financial aid, virtual students face other obstacles off site, with notices and email communications sent to residential students, but not to those at a distance and lectures and other activities that are impossible to attend if you're not on campus. Out of sight, out of mind.

"Universities must think strategically about remote students," Bellantuono advised, recommending an online support office, staffed by an advocate who represents them everywhere on campus—at the bursar's, student aid, bookstore, and elsewhere.

"To be completely accessible remotely, schools must move everything online," she concluded.

While residential students are often encouraged to enroll in more than two or three classes per semester to speed them through to graduation, that's often a big mistake for virtual learners. At NYU, we learned very quickly that remote students don't do well taking more than two courses per semester. Work and family obligations often undermine their studies, leading to a cascade of failures and dropouts.

New online leaders may not have thought deeply about what remote students need or how to help them succeed. Chances are not one in a hundred university presidents or provosts has taken an online class or taught one. Removed from the pressing demands of distant learners, senior academic officers rarely add even a sliver of a line item in their academic spreadsheets to cover virtual student services.

POST-INDUSTRIAL ECONOMY

If you're wondering why online learning is booming, take a look at the latest U.S. Department of Labor figures in the following graph, showing heightened demand for skilled workers (Brundage, 2017). Those with an undergraduate or advanced degree now represent about forty percent of the nation's workforce, while those with just a high school diploma have slipped in the last 25 years from more than a third to about a quarter of American workers.

The graph is a vivid illustration of the present condition of economic life in America. The nation has been fiercely transformed into a post-industrial society in which accelerating technology has cast off large numbers of factory laborers but hasn't created enough new jobs in the service sector or in information-based roles to fill the gap (Lyotard, 1984).

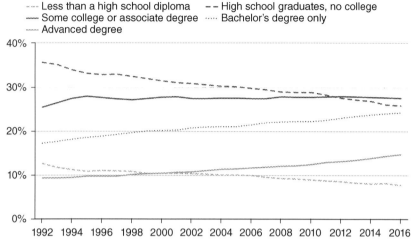

FIGURE 3.1 Education Attainment of U.S. Workforce. The trend lines for those with undergraduate and advanced degrees show a steady rise in prosperity, while the lines for those with no degree sink rapidly downward. Since 2012, workers with some college or higher education now make up the largest share of the U.S. civilian labor force.

Source: Brown (2016)

The clear message for employees who stay in the workforce without a college degree is that their future options are limited. Eventually, they may find themselves out of work altogether.

To escape that harsh outcome, workers without a college degree who are looking to advance must take a stab at enrolling at their nearest college campus or turn to one of the growing numbers of online degree programs. Logistically, it is often difficult or impossible for working adults to get to traditional campuses to pursue degrees, which makes those online options so attractive. America's thirst for a highly skilled workforce is driving the expansion of digital learning. Recent data from the nation's residential colleges show a decline in enrollment, while online is surging at its fastest pace in memory (Ubell, 2018).

In the last century, you didn't need a college degree to get a decent job. A high school diploma was more than enough. In Chelsea, my neighborhood in Manhattan, an elevated railroad that fed hungry factories along the Hudson until 1980 has been turned into a nature walk, with its steel tracks marking flower beds dancing with exotic blooms. Galleries and high-end condos have evicted assembly lines that stretched alongside the old railway. Elsewhere in the U.S., other factory neighborhoods have not been so lucky, debased by crumbling warehouses and defeated production facilities.

My father, a tailor from Poland without a high school diploma, worked productively for years in a men's clothing factory—in what was then called the "needle trades"—not far from my current apartment. Today, without a college education, but armed with his old-world mastery, his chances of earning a good living would be pretty poor.

Today's vastly transformed economy requires workers with post-industrial skills. One website recommends that the best jobs are in high-tech—cloud computing, artificial intelligence, user-experience design, natural language processing, and software testing, among others (Anderson, 2020). It's a rare high school graduate who commands any of these. Luckily, college students who graduate without science and technology degrees, have a chance at finding a job in the new economy if they can demonstrate other in-demand "soft skills"—creativity, collaboration, adaptability, time management, and leadership. Forget driving rivets, welding, or—like my father—cutting men's suit patterns.

In the digital economy, not every discipline guarantees that students will get a good job upon graduation. Not every field offers robust prospects. Depressingly, enrollment in history, philosophy, literature (my major in college), and other departments has been falling for decades. Some colleges are closing liberal arts programs and a cascade of small liberal arts colleges have gone under (Marcus, 2018).

For adult workers, going to school online is not a walk in the park. Faced with on-the-job stress, family obligations, and common day-to-day struggles, many have difficulty hitting the books. For those who were in school long ago, the discipline, time management, and culture of academic life can be daunting.

Even so, for workers with a high school diploma eager to move up, the Labor Department trends show that studying online to earn a degree is a good bet.

It's in the best interest of economically distressed students that higher education makes online learning work; that online students not only toss their mortarboards up in the air at graduation, but go on afterward to lead solid, productive lives.

Getting a degree seems more urgent than ever in today's economy—a curious American alchemy that turns a sheepskin into gold and a chance at happiness.

Comparing the lifetime potential earning power of students who graduate from high school to those who earn a bachelor's degree, a U.S. Census

40 Theory and Practice

Bureau report calculates that over an adult's working life, a college degree is worth nearly twice what a high school diploma is worth—or $2.1 million, compared with $1.2 million (Longley, 2019). A very cool extra million.

In addition to more money, a college degree yields dramatically more meaningful social dividends for graduates—better career opportunities, greater job security, higher work satisfaction, and employee benefits. And studies have shown that college completion correlates with other, more subtle psychological and personal effects—deeper self-worth, better health, and not least, greater personal satisfaction (Faber, 2020).

If virtual education fails to succeed with poor students, then it will merely replicate the severe economic imbalance that is already the shame of the nation's campuses. Online will merely emerge as yet another luxury product for America's privileged students.

Better to fix online for underserved students by making sure instructional design is at its best, that online students make reasonable decisions about their course load, and that higher education recognizes its obligation to provide serious, high-touch services for its remote students. Colleges need to remain as mindful for their online students—if not more supportive—as they are for their residential students.

REFERENCES

Anderson, B. (2020, January 9). The Most In-Demand Hard and Soft Skills of 2020. *LinkedIn Talent Blog.* Retrieved from https://business.linkedin.com/talent-solutions/blog/trends-and-research/2020/most-in-demand-hard-and-soft-skills

Belkin, J. (2018, April 12). Online Courses Associated with Improved Retention. *Campus Technology.* Retrieved from https://campustechnology.com/articles/2018/04/12/research-online-courses-associated-with-improved-retention-access.aspx

Brown, A. (2016). *Key Findings About the American Workforce and the Changing Job Market.* Washington, DC: Pew Research Center.

Brundage, V. (2017). *Profile of Labor Force by Educational Attainment.* Washington, DC: U.S. Bureau of Labor Statistics. Retrieved May 23, 2020, from www.bls.gov/spotlight/2017/educational-attainment-of-the-labor-force/home.htm

Duffin, E. (2020). Community Colleges in the United States. *Statistica.* Retrieved May 21, 2020, from www.statista.com/topics/3468/community-colleges-in-the-united-states/

Dynarski, S. (2018, January 19). Online Courses Are Harming Students Who Need the Most Help. *New York Times.*

Faber, S. (2020). Positive Effects of College Degrees. *The Classroom.*

Fain, P. (2019, May 23). Wealth's Influence on Enrollment and Completion. *Inside Higher Ed.*

Jaggars, D. X. (2011). *Online and Hybrid Course Enrollment and Performance in Washington State Community and Technical Colleges*. New York: Teachers College, Columbia University.

Longley, R. (2019, October 20). Lifetime Earnings Soar with Education. *ThoughtCo*. Retrieved from https://www.thoughtco.com/lifetime-earnings-soar-with-education-3321730

Lyotard, J. F. (1984). *The Postmodern Condition*. Minneapolis: University of Minnesota Press.

Marcus, J. (2018, May 15). *With Enrollment Sliding, Liberal Arts Colleges Struggle to Make a Case for Themselves*. Hechinger Report. Retrieved from https://hechingerreport.org/with-enrollment-sliding-liberal-arts-colleges-struggle-to-make-a-case-for-themselves/

Means, B. (2010). *Evaluation of Evidence-Based Practices in Online Learning: A Meta-Analysis and Review of Online Learning Studies*. Washington, DC: U.S. Department of Education.

National Center for Education Statistics. (2019). *The Condition of Education*. Washington, DC: National Center for Education Statistics.

Piketty, T. (2017). *Capital in the Twenty-First Century*. Cambridge, MA: Harvard University Press.

Shea, P. and T. Bidjerano. (2014). Does Online Learning Impede Degree Completion? A National Study of Community College Students. *Computers & Education*, 75, 103–110.

Swan, K. (2019, December 10). James J. Stukel Distinguished Professor of Educational Leadership, University of Illinois (R. Ubell, Interviewer).

Ubell, R. (2018, January 18). Will Online Ever Conquer Higher Ed? *EdSurge*.

Xu, S. S. (2010). *Online Learning in the Virginia Community College System*. New York: Community College Research Center, Columbia University.

4

Adaptive Learning

As with a pinwheel set in motion, insights from many disciplines—artificial intelligence, cognitive science, linguistics, educational psychology, and data analytics—have come together to form a relatively new field known as learning science, propelling advances in a relatively new personalized practice, adaptive learning.

Designed to adjust in real-time to each student's prior knowledge and skill attainment, adaptive systems respond to variations in ability and diverse student backgrounds, sensitive to the unique needs of each learner. Based on each student's actions, when a student gets stuck, the system automatically suggests strategies on how to get out of it and proceed to mastery.

It turns out that adaptive systems are neither the best thing since sliced bread nor half-baked. Alfred Essa, a Simon Fellow at Carnegie Mellon, says that "in some domains, well-designed adaptive tutors are on a par with human tutors." A truly remarkable feat. Until recently, Essa was head of research at McGraw-Hill.

Like much of edtech, research results can be ambiguous, with some saying adaptive systems are marginally better than conventional classroom teaching, while others report impressive results (VanLehn, 2011). In a recent annual Campus Computing Survey (Campus Computing Project, 2018), a majority of academic chief information officers (CIOs) concluded that "adaptive technology has great potential to improve learning outcomes."

MERGERS AND ACQUISITIONS

In a recent rush, more than half a dozen adaptive learning companies have been scooped up like M&Ms at a candy counter. One of the most notable is Knewton, whose assets were acquired by Wiley. Earlier, Carnegie Learning, Acrobatiq, Knowre and Fishtree were all swallowed in acquisition fever. Meanwhile, ACT, the nonprofit college admission test company, invested $7.5 million in Smart Sparrow.

Edtech guru Phil Hill, widely followed on his *Phil on EdTech* blog, told me that most sales were made, not from strength, but "from positions of weakness and need."

Recent acquisitions give long-term critics a chance, not merely to smirk, but to go in for the kill. After years of predicting that adaptive was a fool's game, with no chance of delivering on what developers promised, what better time than to kick it when it's down? One critical observer (Warner, 2019) admits to "a certain schadenfreude."

With the discovery of fire, believers and skeptics began their interminable heated debates over innovation. For the defense, flames cook your meals, heat your homes, and fire your pots. On the attack, defeatists say they could burn everything down. And so it has been since the web first opened edtech gates in the nineteen-seventies when adaptive learning—also known in its early days as "intelligent tutoring systems"—caught the fire of pioneers who had a hunch that computers might eventually achieve the human ability to adjust individually to each learner's struggles. In the recent adaptive industry shakeout, some vendors are still cooking; others have been snuffed out.

While not as economically momentous, say, as consolidation in the automotive industry, recent adaptive mergers and acquisitions reveal a distinctive pattern. Following a *Harvard Business Review* analysis of corporate consolidation, adaptive systems now mark a stage at which top players own the lion's share of the market, with McGraw-Hill's ALEKS software, acquired in the last decade, leading the pack (Deans et al., 2002).

"Ultimately, a company's long-term success depends on how well it rides the consolidation curve," cautions *Harvard Business Review*. "Slower [growing] firms eventually become acquisition targets and will likely disappear."

The shakeout also parallels the "disillusionment phase" of the Gartner hype cycle, a popular analysis, charting ups and downs of new technologies, coined by Gartner, the big information technology consulting firm. In this treacherous cycle, "Producers of the technology shake out or fail. Investment continues only if the surviving providers improve their products to the satisfaction of early adopters."

44   Theory and Practice

So, what's happening? Why is the adaptive industry house-cleaning, sweeping up some early, promising start-ups?

"Companies like Knewton and others went straight into black-box algorithms, assuming mastery of what learning data actually means and how students learn," observed Hill. "Their customers were really venture capitalists, not academic programs with real teachers and students."

The biggest lesson is that inventing whiz-bang software is not nearly enough. To succeed, vendors must assemble an adaptive Rubik's Cube, snapping four essentials securely in place. The central one, of course, is brilliantly crafted technology, coupled with a deep reservoir of high-quality content, integrated with shrewd assessment tools, embedded with skilled teacher training at each site—all at scale to secure market share, sustainability, profits, and plugged-in implementation at every campus. Not trivial.

While some were good at this or that, few pulled it all together. The biggest handicap for many is their thin content libraries. "Content is where I expect much of the real money will be made on the internet," wrote Bill Gates in his famous 1996 prescient essay, "Content Is King" (Gates, 1996).

One thing start-ups didn't need was arrogance, especially trumpeting extravagant claims. In 2013, five years after Jose Ferreira launched Knewton, he boasted in *Time* that there will be only one company in the world capable of succeeding at adaptive learning. "I think it's going to be us because we're so far ahead now" (Webley, 2013).

None achieved significant scale, except McGraw-Hill's ALEKS, a math and chemistry tutoring system, and its sister product, SmartBook. ALEKS reports more than 4.5 million unique users in K-12 and higher ed courses. Since 2010, it has generated more than 8.7 billion interactions. In humanities, social sciences, science, and business, the company claims more than 11.8 billion interactions since 2009. McGraw-Hill offers more than eight hundred titles for adaptive users.

The ironic denouement is that an old-line publisher, founded at the end of the nineteenth century, more than one hundred and thirty years ago, outwitted high-tech upstarts, countering modern corporate trends in which whiz kids leave the old guard in the digital dust. Curiously, Knewton, an adaptive falling star, is now in the hands of Wiley, another venerable publisher, founded more than two hundred years ago in 1807.

THERE'S NO SUCCESS LIKE FAILURE

Confronted with a thousand learners in a massive open online course, would you be able to give each your personal attention? It seems a far greater challenge than trying to connect with dozens of dazed students in a giant lecture hall on campus.

Armed with data analytics, virtual courses offer many extraordinary features. Chief among them is that they are capable, not only of mass communication but, counterintuitively, mass personalization as well. Exploiting these seemingly contradictory qualities, MOOCs, massive open online courses, not only offer unparalleled global reach and access, but they are equally capable of whispering into each learner's ear electronically. MOOCs have excelled spectacularly in attracting millions to log on, but once students sign up, MOOCs have been less successful in communicating directly to each learner (see Chapter 7).

To help faculty scale individual responses to massive numbers of learners, computer scientists are giving it a shot. In a test of student coding skills in a machine-learning course, the Next Gen team at Coursera, the biggest MOOC provider, first succeeded in teasing out some twenty to forty coding errors learners commonly make. Students in an experimental section of the course no longer answer multiple-choice questions, as most MOOC learners do, but must now write computer code instead. Immediately after viewing a video lecture, students open a browser, inviting them to build a piece of software, demonstrating mastery. Did they actually understand the lesson or did the video just float right by, as if they were nodding off during a tv commercial?

If their submission reveals they've made a common conceptual coding mistake, a pop-up window appears with a clue, suggesting why they may have made the error. "Like a friend looking over your shoulder, giving immediate feedback associated with your mistake," said Coursera data scientist Zhenghao Chen, a member of the Next Gen team that devised the company's new error-feedback loop. "Students should have a clear idea why they failed," Chen said. "Feedback prompts them to correct their misconceptions, to think along different paths."

In the experiment, Coursera scientists are turning education on its head, asking learners to dig into their failures to appreciate why they are mistaken. Failure is rarely exploited to illuminate why learners go astray. Students are commonly measured by how well they master material, not by how they triumph after struggling to correct their mistakes.

John Dewey, American pragmatist and champion of learning by doing— the forerunner of active learning—once remarked, "Failure is instructive. The person who really thinks learns quite as much from his failures as from his successes" (Dewey, 1910).

Chen and his Next Gen team claim that motivation and perseverance, attributes honed by many in video games, are what learning is often about.

46 Theory and Practice

In *Going Online* (Ubell, 2017), I observed, "Students soon discover that learning is a gradual, often stumbling process that can lead down blind alleys, often hobbled by false starts. Marked by ruptures and dislocations, learning is a risk-taking exercise, not an elegant performance."

Unlike most MOOC learners, those in the Coursera pilot machine-learning class are required to perform real-time operations on the fly, as if they were playing a video game, actively engaged in their own knowledge discovery.

"Active learning is much more effective than just receiving lectures passively," Chen said. "It helps with retention and avoids misconceptions learners stumble over when they don't receive automated feedback."

Chen says that his team's approach increases persistence. Instead of dropping out in frustration, students who get positive feedback eventually succeed in solving problems.

"Learners are not asked to respond with a binary yes-or-no solution, but are asked to apply content from the lecture, reinforcing what they learned," Chen said. "The method encourages learners to gain access to their own mastery, rather than being confused by what they believe they understand."

Angela Duckworth, noted psychologist at the University of Pennsylvania, in her best-selling book, *Grit*, wondered why some talented people frequently fail to reach their potential, while others—far less gifted—often achieve what they set out to attain? Duckworth claims that the secret is the quality of passionate persistence, especially in the face of challenges and setbacks (Duckworth, 2016). A form of psychological strength, grit consists of perseverance of effort and consistency of interest. The adaptive learning methods introduced by Chen and his colleagues encourage and reinforce these qualities.

The great Swiss clinical psychologist Jean Piaget long ago theorized that our thoughts are structured by schema, a framework of preconceived ideas about how the world works (Piaget, 1954). Mired by deeply held mind-sets, no matter how many times learners go back to a video lecture or a textbook, they still may get stuck, failing, exasperatingly, to understand essential concepts.

A famous riddle illustrates conceptual blindness. A father and his son are in a car accident in which the father dies instantly. The son survives, requires surgery, and is taken to a local hospital. Soon a surgeon enters the operating room and says, "I'm afraid I cannot operate on the boy."

"Why not?" a nurse wonders.

"Because he's my son," the doctor responds.

In a number of experiments, most people were so stumped by the puzzle they could not unpack their resistance to the fact that mothers, too, might be surgeons. Similar blindness prevents students from recognizing their own misconceptions.

An early version of the course tested by Chen was first launched as a MOOC in 2011 at Stanford University. To everyone's astonishment, an eye-popping one hundred thousand students enrolled. It featured quizzes and graded programming assignments, ultimately emerging as one of the top MOOCs ever—over time, attracting more than 1.2 million learners.

The instructor of this legendary MOOC is Andrew Ng, former chief scientist at Baidu, the $12 billion Chinese web-services firm, often called the Chinese Google, one of the largest internet companies in the world. In 2012, Ng co-founded Coursera with Daphne Koller and is now chairman.

Coursera is not alone in exploiting big data and other advanced techniques. For example, Sense, a New York-based tech start-up with research and development labs in Tel Aviv, is testing pattern recognition and semantic analysis methods that automatically bundle student answers that exhibit common solutions. In a MOOC, with dozens or even thousands of students, automatic batching allows faculty to pinpoint responses to learners who give fairly similar answers, personalizing faculty-student interaction at scale.

Just as in the Coursera approach, instructors can deliver feedback to resulting clusters. In contrast, however, Sense does not require faculty or subject-matter experts to feed the system with examples of common errors, as in the Coursera experiment. With Sense, instructors may feed fifty or more new quiz solutions at any time; the system then automatically reveals common patterns—successful responses, common mistakes, even novel solutions—that are shared among submissions. In addition to text, the Sense system, like Coursera's, can interpret computer code, but also mathematical equations.

In choosing one of Coursera's most prized courses, the Next Gen team departed from delivering conventional video-streamed lectures—an exhausted pedagogy that has long since outlived its sell-by date. Instead, in their radical experiment, they are embracing a far more innovative active learning style—including digital interactive modules, like the computer code exercise—to lift students off their binge-watching couches, challenging them to face their screens to act and not glaze over.

REFERENCES

Campus Computing Project. (2018). *The 2018 National Survey of eLearning and Information Technology in US Higher Education*. Retrieved from https://www.campuscomputing.net/content/2018/10/31/the-2018-campus-computing-survey

48 Theory and Practice

Deans, G. K. et al. (2002, December). The Consolidation Curve. *Harvard Business Review*, 80.

Dewey, J. (1910). *How We Think*. Boston: D. C. Heath.

Duckworth, A. (2016). *Grit: The Power and Passion of Perseverance*. New York: Scribner.

Gates, B. (1996). *The Road Ahead*. New York: Penguin.

Piaget, J. (1954). *The Construction of Reality in the Child*. New York: Basic Books.

Ubell, R. (2017). *Going Online*. New York: Routledge.

VanLehn, K. (2011, October 17). The Relative Effectiveness of Human Tutoring, Intelligent Tutoring Systems, and Other Tutoring Systems. *Educational Psychologist*, 46.

Warner, J. (2019, May 7). Knewton Is Gone: The Larger Threat Remains. *Inside Higher Ed*.

Webley, K. (2013, June 6). The Adaptive Learning Revolution. *Time*.

Section 3
Scaling-up

5

Academic Digital Economy

The university is often portrayed as a place where young men and women loaf freely on a soft, grassy quad under a noble bell tower. Lecture halls and dormitories circle them, busy with faculty members and students coming and going on campus.

Hovering over this idyllic image is the online campus, where students rarely, if ever, set foot on manicured lawns. Digital students study at home or while commuting to and from work, often late at night after the kids are asleep.

Before the invasion of the internet, the university comprised a secure, single identity; now—with about a third of college students online (Lederman, 2018)—the American college is bifurcated.

When I first entered the virtual university a couple of decades ago, I imagined, apart from instruction, that online and on campus in most respects would be pretty much the same. Surprisingly, just over twenty years later, things didn't turn out that way in practice. Like fraternal twins, online and in-person campuses are the same, but different.

Delivery methods are hardly the only divergence between face-to-face and virtual instruction. A deeper look reveals strikingly different economies and cultures, student populations, status of faculty members, curricula and infrastructure, and even tuition.

DIFFERENT STUDENTS AND FACULTY

Work represents the principal difference that separates digital from face-to-face students. Online, about eighty percent of students work full- or part-time (Learning House, 2019). In glaring contrast, just forty percent of residential students aged sixteen to 25 work full-time (Hussar, 2020), a key economic difference that sets them apart from most academic consequences that follow. It's a tale of two cities, with mostly middle-class, eighteen-year-old freshman taking seats on campus, while adult men and women (often more women than men), many married with children at home, occupy most virtual slots. And online students are more likely than on-campus students to be the first in their families to go to college.

In other words, the digital university welcomes older, working, nontraditional learners (Johnson, 2019) who gravitate to online degrees to overcome workforce obstacles that prevent many without a degree from earning their fair share in today's often-bewildering, post-industrial economy (Lyotard, 1984) (see Chapter 3).

"The fastest growing population in higher education is adult learners, now comprising nearly half of the total learner population. Working professionals have vastly different needs than those of the traditional student," said Nelson Baker, dean of professional education at Georgia Tech in an American Council on Education (ACE) report (American Council on Education, 2019), acknowledging that college leaders are uneasy over the inability of conventional higher ed to respond effectively to fierce market forces.

Online faculty members, too, are not drawn from the same pool as those on campus. Physical campuses enlist a growing number of part-time adjunct faculty—which now represent nearly three-quarters of university faculty (American Association of University Professors, 2018)—with a critical mass of full-time and tenured professors. But the situation online tilts far more to adjuncts, with very likely ninety percent or more in that category.

Digging as hard as I could, I could not find reliable data revealing how many contingent instructors teach online. But from my own experience, and from my knowledge of hiring practices at for-profit and nonprofit schools with large online student enrollments (where little or no research is conducted), the number of full-time faculty teaching online is very thin, and at some colleges, very likely close to zero.

Part-time faculty teaching online represent an unsettling trend, not only in virtual education, but in residential colleges, too—a troubling shift in higher education that has introduced a professional class system that cultivates elite status for full-time, tenure-track faculty, with generous compensation, benefits, and support, leaving part-time, contingent faculty out on a limb, with meager compensation, little or no benefits, and often frail support.

The transformation of the professoriate from mostly full-time faculty to itinerant labor goes back many years. In 1969, roughly 78 percent of U.S. faculty held tenure or tenure-track positions. Adjuncts accounted for only about 22 percent (Kezar and Maxey, 2013). Today, full-time and adjunct employment at the nation's campuses has completely reversed, with adjuncts occupying the lion's share and full-time faculty a more modest slice.

Looking back, the university introduced the gig economy long before Uber and Lyft, exposing three-quarters of its workforce to fragile economic vulnerability. According to a recent study from American Federation of Teachers, before the pandemic, 25 percent of adjuncts were dependent on federal assistance. A third earned less than $25,000 a year, below federal poverty levels, earning between $2,000 and $7,000 a class (Schanzer, 2020). As expected, when layoffs shook the nation's campuses in response to the coronavirus, adjuncts were among the first to go.

DIFFERENT INFRASTRUCTURE AND MARKETING INVESTMENTS

A key difference between the residential campus and its online sibling is infrastructure. A conventional college requires enormous investments in soft, grassy grounds. Add security, dormitories, parking, gyms, cafeterias, heat and snow removal in winter, air-conditioning in summer—let alone classrooms, labs, and sports facilities—and the burden is often far more than what is required to support a luxury resort. Online, operating only in the air above, without a physical campus below, academic investments are limited to less than a handful of budget lines—instruction, course design, and edtech software.

For years, many observers wondered when the digital revolution would overrun the university as it has commerce elsewhere. In my neighborhood in Manhattan—and in cities and towns across America—mom-and-pop shops and even national brand stores are collapsing, as if swept away by hurricane Katrina. Amazon's indifferent digital finger has carelessly pushed most of them over. While the academic economy has not been as severely shaken yet, the recent ACE report warns that the inability of American higher ed to respond effectively may have equally disruptive consequences in the future.

When the Sloan Foundation first moved to stimulate digital education at the nation's colleges and universities more than a quarter of a century

54 Scaling-up

ago, it christened online learning as "asynchronous learning networks," an eccentric name for what is now known simply as online learning. Since it was in its very early days, Sloan had no idea what to call it; but it surely bet on a winning horse.

Eventually, the foundation invested nearly $75 million in institutions willing to test electronic teaching to see if it worked (Sloan Foundation, 2009). I received some of that largess about twenty years ago in grants to launch virtual master's degrees, among the very first in the nation, when I was dean of "web-based distance learning" at Stevens Institute of Technology in Hoboken, NJ.

At Sloan-sponsored summer workshops in upstate New York, early in this century, I listened eagerly to pioneering faculty who imagined that virtual classes would be taught with radical education methods that had been proposed earlier by giants in progressive education—John Dewey, Jean Piaget, and Paulo Freire, among others (Ubell, 2009). The idea was to deliver digital instruction as a student-centered, peer-to-peer, active-learning practice.

Today, while education reform is still on the nation's academic agenda, these days many colleges going online are doing so for economic reasons. Virtual education is now seen as a way to bring in new students—and therefore new revenue—as students in traditional programs have become harder to come by. At high-level strategy sessions at conference tables in president's and provost's offices at colleges across the country, academic leaders are not commonly arguing over the pedagogical merits of constructivist education theories but are anxiously calculating how to go online without going under (see Chapter 2).

In the roughly two decades over which virtual instruction has evolved—initially run by online amateurs (like me) in experiments dotting the country—few participating institutions expected to generate sizable financial returns. We were all tinkering with what worked and what didn't. Pedagogy was more on our minds than profits.

When online was first introduced as a pedagogical advance, faculty members often rose up against it—or more often, just ignored it, the most devastating form of resistance (Ubell, 2017). If it weren't for economic necessity, online might not have grown to the force it has today. Of course, in the 2020 pandemic, online mushroomed so that nearly all college students in the U.S. were online (see Chapter 1).

In the nineteen seventies and eighties, when Wall Street got wind of the billions to be made from government-backed loans for tuition, for-profits hit the jackpot (McGuire, 2012). To some extent, the boom in online learning that rose before the pandemic was a consequence of traditional colleges

Academic Digital Economy   55

following the enterprising techniques introduced by for-profits who left small-scale institutions in the dust. For-profits were happy to build giant education factories with thousands of online students (see Chapter 12).

Inevitably, nonprofit institutions were forced to adopt for-profit marketing strategies when state legislatures withdrew support for public universities (Pew Charitable Trusts, 2009) and when, for some small colleges, idyllic Jeffersonian campuses could no longer be sustained.

Thoughtful academic faculty are urging new online initiatives to be built on a foundation of student-centered active learning, even as digital education increases scale. In *Learning and the Future of Higher Education*, Joshua Kim of Dartmouth College, and Edward Maloney of Georgetown University, argue that the broader introduction of digital education across the nation creates even more opportunities for active learning to be adopted (Kim, 2020).

And to my surprise, even as virtual education balloons, those giant online programs at nonprofit colleges are trying imaginative digital alternatives to deliver virtual peer-to-peer, active learning. Except that they are doing it at a scale unimaginable to those attending Sloan workshops decades ago.

SCALING-UP

Small doesn't cut it anymore, at least not at picturesque independent colleges, largely in rural New England and the Midwest. Over the last decade, nearly fifty colleges that once represented a pastoral ideal of American higher education, have vanished, discarded from their arcadian place in academia (Seltzer, 2017b).

A couple of years ago, the Memphis College of Art, a private institution in Tennessee, announced it was closing, following the death march of dozens of failing schools. When I read the news, I shook my head in disbelief when I learned that the school had enrolled merely 307 students—shockingly fewer than were seated in just one giant lecture hall at Columbia University when I audited a freshman cell biology class many years ago.

"We expect that there will be more college closures over the next three to four years," Susan Fitzgerald, a senior vice president at Moody's, told *MarketWatch* (Berman, 2015). "I don't think it's going to be a landslide of college closures, but we are coming through a very tough period of time."

At public universities, the continuing withdrawal of higher education funding by state legislators is destabilizing state universities, forcing them to turn elsewhere for support. "State funding of public universities is on a track to reach zero in less than twenty years in some states and as soon as six

56 Scaling-up

in Colorado and nine in Alaska," warned Jane Karr, former "Education Life" editor of *The New York Times*, (Karr, 2017). The troubling decline is likely to accelerate, fueled by relatively flat high school graduation rates, squeezing many small private schools, gasping for survival (Zinshteyn, 2016).

Small, private American colleges may face even more uneasy futures after the coronavirus pandemic. An analytical model, developed by Boston start-up Edmit, found that more than a third of private, four-year colleges are at high risk (Edmit, 2020). "Many colleges will be able to find ways to survive this crisis, but others will need to make the incredibly difficult decision to seek a merger or close in the next few years," Edmit co-founder Nick Ducoff predicted (Thys, 2020).

Edmit analyzed seventeen years of tuition revenue, return on investment, expenses, and tuition discounts offered by 937 colleges. If present financial trends continue, the model estimated that 345 will be at high risk, forecasting that they may not survive the next six years.

Even before the global pandemic, which left many colleges skating on very thin financial ice, higher education was already under stress. As Moody's, the big rating agency, reported—even as it upgraded higher ed from negative to stable in 2019—"Over the longer term, social risks will continue to transform the U.S. higher education sector," citing declining enrollments and hesitant college officers, reluctant to move rapidly online (Moody's Investment Service, 2019). Just a few months later, however, with COVID-19 shutting down the nation's campuses, Moody's reversed its rating to negative (Moody's Investment Service, 2020), predicting, "The coronavirus outbreak will negatively affect higher education for the next year as universities worldwide grapple with lower student demand and lost income" (see Chapter 1).

Clayton Christensen, the late Harvard business guru, applying his theory of disruptive innovation to higher education (Christensen and Eyring, 2011), was certain that digital incursions in colleges and universities would so rapidly undermine our shaky campuses that as many as half of American colleges would close in the next ten to fifteen years. His theory claimed that once cheaper and commonly inferior innovations are introduced in the marketplace, they tend to supplant market leaders from their dominant position, serving consumers better.

But like the wolf in the children's fable, no matter how much Christensen huffed and puffed about his theory, most universities remain standing, like the sturdy brick house built by the cleverest of the little pigs. Sadly, quite a number of colleges have failed in the last decades (Education Dive, 2020), but none have succumbed to Christensen's forces of disruptive innovation.

Dwindling high school graduates is the chief ill wind to blow them down. Brutal tuition increases have also chased away many who can no longer afford to enroll.

For a time, the idea of disruptive innovation was quite fashionable in business and academic circles, but flaws in the theory and lack of evidence burst its balloon, especially following devastating critiques in *The New Yorker* (Lapore, 2014) and the *MIT Sloan Business Review* (King and Baatartogtkh, 2015). While a number of scholars feared the destructive winds of digital education, to others the theory seemed far less applicable in higher ed, especially since online learning played a very limited role for decades from the time it was first introduced at the turn of this century.

Not one college has gone under owing to the rise of digital education in the academic marketplace. Ironically, virtual instruction did not put the university out of business; on the contrary, it saved it—especially when the coronavirus threatened to close down the nation's campuses (see Chapter 1).

Apart from hoped-for pedagogical innovations, the big promise of online education was that it would help unlock the nation's financial academic choke hold. The scale of the internet, just as it has bent the economic laws of most industries, would rescue institutions from the financial troubles facing our colleges.

It turned out that the first major experiment in internet education— online classes—didn't do much to loosen the classroom economic squeeze. Virtual classes were mostly stuck in the locked jaws of the same student-faculty ratio as on campus, with small classes of merely twenty to fifty students. For a time, online economic promise never really took off.

For years, the only thing that digital instruction changed was that it opened new markets. Students could now go online from outside the campus neighborhood, from just about anywhere—Indiana, Istanbul, and beyond—enrolling without occupying beds in a dorm or parking spots in a campus lot.

Colleges and universities have juggled with academic productivity and pricing, hoping to solve their financial troubles in three treacherous ways— increasing the number of students per faculty member, crowding students into giant lecture halls, reducing labor costs by exchanging expensive tenured faculty with a much cheaper itinerant workforce, and precariously, raising tuition beyond already extravagant prices. More schools have been killed by the cruel cost of faculty teaching empty seats in thinning classrooms. The Memphis College of Art employed 37 full-time faculty for 307 students. You do the math.

58   Scaling-up

"Scaling is absolutely critical for higher education institutions in today's marketplace. Through scaling, institutions can 'do more with less'—they can meet the sky-high expectations of today's discerning students while keeping their costs and prices low," comments *EvoLLLution* magazine (Rawls, 2020).

Online also opened colleges and universities to local and distant midcareer adults, representing a gurgling new revenue stream, flooded by students who, because of demanding work and family life, cannot attend classes at nearby campuses. Otherwise, the tech revolution, which had powered the digital transformation of most of today's economy, had not liberated higher education from its small-scale cottage industry paralysis.

When I first launched online programs at New York University, an insightful computer science professor, who was quite supportive of what I was up to, nevertheless doubted the long-term economic benefit of online education, wondering how many more students I could enroll in an online class than on campus. I responded that to assure quality education, class size would be about the same. "In that case," he warned, "online will never offer significant economic advantages over face-to-face."

After two decades, new federal data show that six million U.S. college students now take one or more distance education courses—or more than a quarter of all U.S. students. Until recently, virtual students racked up double-digit gains, year after year, far outpacing no-growth, residential numbers. It's one of the great American higher education success stories (Seaman et al., 2018).

Eager to uncover what's happening, investigators check off five common market forces they say account for most fluctuations—declining demographics, showing a shrinking U.S. college-age population; troubling rates of family income inequality, forcing away many from poor and middle income families; an improving job market (before the pandemic), attracting greater numbers to a more accommodating workplace; rising numbers of adult learners; and, crucially for digital education, stiff competition, with dozens of new virtual programs chasing after fewer and fewer students.

Plus, there is a new competitive intruder: MOOCs. With MOOCs giving away college courses to potential customers, the result is certain to have a depressing effect on college' sales. We'll never know how many of the one hundred and ten million learners who took a free ride on MOOCs would have enrolled in university courses and paid tuition for the privilege. MOOCs have demonstrated that there is a huge reservoir of internet fans out there, taking MOOC courses at Coursera, edX, and other providers, passing by local campuses (see Chapter 7).

These and other marketplace factors effect both on-campus and online enrollments, but they've been hammering the residential population brutally, bleeding more than 250,000 on-campus students nationwide by fall 2015. Were it not for online, Jeff Seaman, co-director of the Babson Survey Research Group, producer of the widely followed annual survey on virtual education and the Digital Learning Compass report, told me that the total loss of the nation's university population would have exceeded one million in 2015 over the previously reported year.

SUPPLY AND DEMAND

While fluctuations are commonly attributed to demand—increasing or decreasing numbers of customers purchasing your product—surprisingly little attention has been given to supply; that is, the flow of new offerings in university course catalogs. Studying the digital education economy with your finger on the scale of the marketplace tends to unbalance the equation. With a heavy hand on sales and little or no attention paid to production, observers may be led down a blind alley. Andy Grove, founder and former chief executive officer (CEO) of Intel, famously said, "The internet doesn't change everything. It doesn't change supply and demand" (Griffen, 2016).

If the demand side of the enrollment equation is treacherous, the supply side is equally charged. Take, for example, faculty resistance to online instruction, a serious obstacle to filling the pipeline of new online courses— a production barrier economists call occupational labor shortage. The obstacle to growth is often not accreditation—which can sometimes be rocky—but stubborn faculty opposition to going online. Nearly all schools face faculty resistance, slowing the entrance of new online courses (Ubell, 2017).

Looking back to the early days of web-based distance learning, online programs behaved like new start-ups with skyrocketing products. Early-to-market digital courses were not only fulfilling pent-up demand, but with the opening of the digital academic pipeline, streams of new virtual courses flooded learners with entirely new brainy products never accessible before. At first, socially motivated faculty rushed in, eager to deliver digital classes that promised active-learning benefits—virtual teamwork, peer-to-peer learning, and other progressive, constructivist practices. Over the first decades, they tested new teaching and learning methods, spearheading booming growth.

Karen Pollack, vice provost for online education at Penn State World Campus, recalled,

60 Scaling-up

> In the early days, faculty who went online believed in the transformative power of online learning because it provided greater student access. Early adopters did not see technology as a barrier, but rather as an enabler. Today, few faculty or administrators ask how they can go online. They are not convinced it's something they ought to do.

New courses are now launched with an eye toward preparing students for post-industrial careers in business and STEM fields, with classes introduced less with the intellectually innovative zeal of first movers than with savvy spreadsheet calculation.

In those early days, online faculty were often sent off into cyberspace with a computer, a passcode, and a stack of PowerPoints, with little or no preparation. Today, digital instructors enter their virtual classrooms, not as autonomous teachers, but commonly as part of a team, partnering with instructional designers, videographers, and game specialists, among other experts, driving up the cost of entry (see Chapter 2).

Schools can no longer waltz into digital education with meager budgets but must make serious investments to achieve the right balance of high-performance learning technologies with astute virtual pedagogy, aiming to satisfy heightened and more knowing online students. When university financial officers anxiously weigh benefits against risks, inevitably, the digital engine slows.

Supply also retreats when for-profits close and government withdraws its support. Over the last few years, about a hundred for-profits fell off the radar in the wake of President Obama's jaundiced view of predatory, corporate-run higher ed, chopping nearly three percent off digital enrollments from the previous year's results. For example, the University of Phoenix lost nearly two hundred thousand online enrollments between 2013 and 2016. For-profit retrenchment dealt a damaging blow to online numbers. It's quite a turnabout when nonprofits come out on top and big corporations suffer serious injury. Still, for-profits have not flamed out yet. The pandemic has stimulated new interest in them, owing to their greater flexibility and other attractions for working adults. In the crisis, enrollments have gone up.

BLENDED LEARNING

The surprising news in the digital supply chain is the surge of blended (or hybrid) learning. Offered partly on campus and partly online, blended courses satisfy a fired-up demand for flipped classrooms, low-residency programs, digital labs, and flex delivery. As Joel Hartman, recently retired

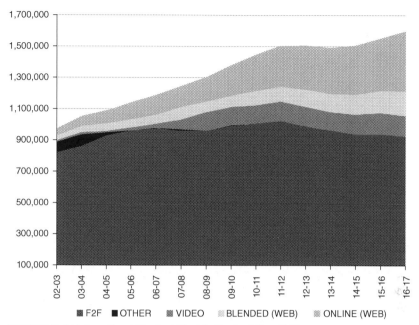

FIGURE 5.1 University of Central Florida Student Credit Hours
Source: University of Central Florida

vice president for information technologies and resources and CIO at the University of Central Florida (UCF) in Orlando, acknowledges, "Digital education is no longer one thing, but a continuum."

Take a look at UCF's graph, representing student credit hours, to see where the steam is rising. Just as in the national trend, UCF's face-to-face (F2F) numbers are falling, but unlike enrollments reported elsewhere, online at UCF is steaming ahead, pretty much paralleling the movement at other large state universities, where growth continues to outperform the rest of the country by more than thirteen percent. In what seems like a contradiction, residential numbers have also climbed as on-campus students occupy virtual seats in blended courses.

The hidden news is that UCF's (and other schools') dramatic bands of rising blended and other courses are buried, not counted in the data released by the U.S. Department of Education's Integrated Postsecondary Education Data System (IPEDS), the nation's primary source of college and university statistics. By not calculating the contribution of blended, we're ignoring one of the most significant trends in higher education today. The UCF

62 Scaling-up

chart confirms the quite surprising existence of a quiet revolution in virtual instruction in which blended is penetrating the often-hermetic walls of conventional classrooms. As online learning observer Michael Horn notes in *Forbes*, "Blended delivery of online learning doesn't count toward the data" (Horn, 2015).

Students enrolled in blended courses are the undocumented citizens of digital education. As the UCF chart shows, blended represents the largely unacknowledged next generation of the academic economy.

DIGITAL RECRUITMENT

With the invasion of internet marketing—first introduced cynically by for-profits and then imitated vigorously by MOOCs and online program managers (OPMs), an entirely unexpected source of funding emerged (see Chapters 6 and 7). Until supercharged digital recruitment blew in, online recruitment was more like a hand-cranked machine than a jet engine.

With MOOCs, the promise of the internet's marketing power came into its own. Since they were launched in the last decade, more than one hundred million learners have signed up (Shah, 2019). The pandemic has pushed enrollment at greater speed, with Coursera, the largest MOOC provider, reporting that ten million learners were taking its courses in a single, thirty-day period during the COVID-19 crisis in the spring of 2020, a stunning 644 percent increase over the previous, nonpandemic spring. For comparison, the total number enrolled in all U.S. public and private colleges and universities today is about 20.4 million (Statista, 2020).

"Digital marketing has experienced the most significant revolution over recent times, with university brands, leaders and marketing departments now faced with a dizzying array of tools and techniques," Stuart Branbery, marketing manager at SocialSignIn, wrote at *LinkedIn Pulse* (Branbery, 2015).

According to Arizona State University President Michael M. Crow, state universities must make a significant adjustment in capacity in order to educate the next generation of the U.S. workforce. That's why ASU is forging ahead to get to two hundred thousand students in less than a decade—numbers we haven't seen since the heyday of for-profits. Crow confirmed,

> We have set a goal of enrolling a hundred thousand online and distance learners by 2025. Projections through 2024 for on-campus undergrad enrollment are approximately eighty thousand and

on-campus graduate enrollment is approximately twelve thousand five hundred. Our mission with respect to enrollment over all is to provide affordable access to all who qualify for admission.

"The Iron Triangle is a nineteenth-century idea," Crow said, referring to the three sides of the fierce demands of higher education—quality, access, and cost—that have crushed many institutions (Crow, 2017). Crow claims that the aggressive immersion of technology in all aspects of student and faculty life—as well as cutting many courses down to seven and half weeks, with the same credit as the common fifteen weeks—plus other academic innovations, has made rapid, quality growth possible.

TUITION STRATEGIES

Classic economic theory predicts that when demand falls, so do prices. But when it comes to the price of college in the past few decades, it's been just the other way around. As data from the National Student Clearinghouse Center shows, tuition has escalated even as enrollments fell (National Student Clearinghouse, 2017).

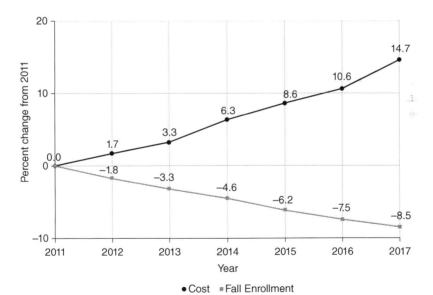

FIGURE 5.2 Rising Tuition, Falling Enrollment
Source: Jaschik (2015)

64 Scaling-up

The dispiriting result is that half of all low income high school graduates, cowed by sticker shock, don't even bother to fill out applications to go to college. A report by the American Council on Education concludes, "The rapid price increases in recent years, especially in the public college sector, may have led many students, particularly low income students, to think that college is out of reach financially."

Responding to the challenge, a few universities are finally reversing course or slowing tuition increases, either stepping on the breaks or tossing out tuition altogether. One of the most dramatic examples comes from NYU's Medical School, which ended its $55,000 yearly tuition in 2018, at a cost to the school of about $24 million annually (Seltzer, 2018).

When I first came across this striking news, I hesitated to imagine that NYU's action might be a harbinger. But after digging into recent news reports, I discovered that NYU's move was not an outlier. A handful of colleges have eliminated fees, others have frozen tuition, and many others sliced tuition like lunch meat at a deli counter. Mills College, for example, a small San Francisco Bay area liberal arts college, chopped $25,000 off tuition (Krupnick, 2018). About twenty other schools have reduced tuition, from a 42 percent cut at Utica College in New York, to five percent at Washington State University (Pitsker, 2015). I wondered if it was the start of an academic Costco movement.

Unfortunately, the reality is a bit more complicated, and not always a better deal for students. Some colleges, it turns out, are using a curious academic sleight-of-hand known as "tuition resets" to make changes that look like discounts but sometimes aren't. That's the argument made by Rick Seltzer in his thorough investigation of deceptive college pricing techniques (Seltzer, 2017a).

In his *Inside Higher Ed* piece, Seltzer argued that,

> resets typically aren't being used as a mechanism to cut the net price
> a private college or university charges—the net price being what
> students and their families actually pay after colleges lower the sticker
> price by offering grants and scholarships.

Seltzer recognized that many recent cuts are merely marketing flags, fluttering as in a used car lot, broadcasting lower prices, signaling that "an institution is affordable—a way to grab students' attention and tell them they really can find a way to pay for a private college." But as some colleges lower tuition, they also cut financial aid, leaving students and their families stuck with exactly the same bill as they would have paid before the misleading cut.

Tuition resets reveal that academic leaders, especially at schools that are watching apprehensively as enrollments dip, fear that mushrooming resistance may eventually put them out of business.

Luckily for many students, some discounts are real—and promising. St. John's University, with campuses in Santa Fe, NM and Annapolis, MD, is cutting tuition from $52,000 to $35,000, rending a deep gash in the college's finances. To make up for the loss, the university plans to generate $300 million in a fundraising campaign.

Mark Roosevelt, college-wide president of St. John's College and president of the Santa Fe campus, said in one report,

> We believe the days when students and families could pay exorbitant tuition prices are gone and they aren't coming back—nor should they—and we are placing philanthropy at the center of our financial model rather than student-derived revenue to ensure we remain strong financially as a college.
>
> (Valbrun, 2018)

St. Johns is not alone in turning to philanthropy to cut or eliminate tuition. Fundraising also made it possible for the NYU Medical School to enroll students tuition-free. Uptown, Columbia University's Vagelos College of Physicians and Surgeons replaced all student financial aid packages with grants made possible with resources in a new fund launched with a $150 million donation (Berman, 2018).

Recently, a wealthy real-estate developer donated millions to the University of Hawaii to make the institution tuition-free eventually (Candid, 2017). Donors also funded Brown University with enough cash to do away with student loans entirely. Among other institutions using philanthropy to ease tuition hikes, donations at Arkansas State University made it possible for the school to avoid a price increase.

The biggest news in academic philanthropy was the unprecedented $1.3 billion donation from billionaire business leader Michael Bloomberg to Johns Hopkins University, allowing financially strapped incoming students to eliminate federal loans (Scutari, 2018).

While philanthropy is one way to reverse the spiral, it's a tough struggle for many schools. You'd think that with the top one percent of American households now owning forty percent of the country's wealth (Picketty, 2014), raising money from the super-rich would be easy. With such unparalleled deep pockets, these ultra-rich can easily make college affordable for the rest of us. But this group has proved tight-fisted—often giving away less than two percent of their income to charity (Perry, 2013).

66 Scaling-up

As an online dean over two decades, my philosophical position was that there should be no difference between virtual and face-to-face education. To avoid establishing academic class division, with online the bargain-basement poor cousin of the superior designer model on campus, colleges must set the same price, too.

As I argue in *Going Online,*

> By and large, colleges and universities charge the same tuition on campus and online. The practice follows the principle that, if the programs offer the same content, with the same or equally qualified faculty, eventually reporting the same outcomes, there should be no difference in tuition either.
>
> (Ubell, 2017)

But recent examples at a few enterprising colleges have caused me to change my tune.

Eager to attract budget-minded students, online has cautiously entered the discount economy. One of the first schools to offer differential pricing, Berklee College of Music's online tuition, for example, is set at just over a third of the base price for its on-campus degrees (Lieberman, 2018). With online tuition for its bachelor's degree program at nearly $60,000, that's about sixty percent less than the more than $171,000 residential students pay in Boston.

And in a historic shift, the University of Pennsylvania, one of the nation's most-selective schools, launched a nearly fully online bachelor's degree in applied arts and sciences (McKenzie, 2018). It is among the first of the Ivies to offer a virtual undergraduate degree. (Harvard, for example, does not offer a single complete degree online, neither in its master's nor bachelor's degree programs.) In an equally surprising move for a premier institution, UPenn is also giving enrolled students in its new online bachelor's degree program an unprecedented discount—cutting virtual tuition by $1,000 per credit.

As colleges struggle with spiraling tuition, they're testing inventive ways to damp it down without going bust. Boxed-in on campus, some universities have turned to virtual degrees to wriggle out of their tuition squeeze. A number of colleges have partnered with big MOOC providers, principally Coursera and edX, to offer large-scale online courses at far lower prices, in part to attract new students to their higher-priced online and on-campus degrees (see Chapter 7).

Scale is the driving force behind the extraordinary economic advantages of MOOC-based online degrees—mostly at the master's level—that are now available at steep discounts from first-ranked schools from such providers at Coursera and edX. In 2014, Nelson Baker, Georgia Tech's dean of professional education, launched among the very first of these. Baker told me that scale allows the school to offer its digital degree for far less than it charges residential students (Ubell, 2017). Four thousand students are enrolled in the school's online computer science master's degree program, with just three hundred in the on-campus Atlanta program. Georgia residents pay about $20,000 per year for the residential degree, with out-of-staters paying nearly double that. Online students pay an astonishingly low $7,000 per year for a first-class degree.

In partnership with edX, Georgian Tech delivers two more low-cost online master's degrees—one in analytics and another in cybersecurity. Seven others from the University of Texas at Austin, University California at San Diego and other top schools were also announced by edX. Not to be outdone, Coursera, offers 22 discounted master's programs, also from top institutions, with online degrees from the University of Michigan and the University of Illinois, among other schools. Coursera and its MOOC competitors are in a race to emerge as the top provider of discounted online master's degrees and—in a relatively new development—low-cost online bachelor's degrees, too.

Admittedly, on the whole, virtual tuition is largely the same as on campus—occasionally even a bit more expensive. But MOOC-based degrees are just at the starting line of what appears to be a rush to hang discount tags on online degrees.

With enrollment in residential programs stalling, colleges have jettisoned some on-campus programs, replacing them with online delivery only. The University of Illinois Gies School will stop delivering its on-campus MBA, offering its fast-growing online degree instead (Jaschik, 2019). Enrollment in the school's online MBA, launched in 2016, jumped from 114 initially to 1,955 today. The 98 MBA students stranded on campus moved online to complete their degrees. Tuition for the online degree, called an iMBA, is about $22,000. The previous on-campus equivalent was priced at about $80,000.

Efforts by just a handful of schools do not constitute a national discount movement for academic degrees, but taken together, with the news that the nation's knee-jerk annual rise in tuition is stabilizing, there are signs that the spiral may no longer be spinning out of control, releasing a deep sigh of relief from millions soon heading for college. Even before new online experiments and other tuition-slashing movements, U.S. Bureau of Labor Statistics data shows a recent easing of year-after-year increases, with annual growth at its lowest in a decade (U.S. Bureau of Labor Statistics, 2020).

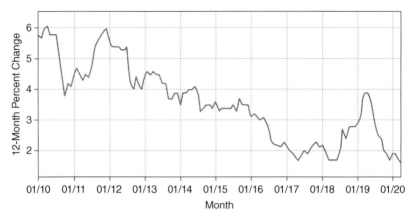

FIGURE 5.3 Declining College Tuition and Fees. In 2010, yearly hikes hovered around six percent. In sharp contrast, a decade later, in 2020, increases tracked as low as 1.6 percent, a sure sign that institutions are getting the picture with tuition creep slowing down—heading to zero?

Source: U.S. Bureau of Labor Statistics

Reversing the tuition spiral is not going to be easy for most schools. Forces that compel colleges and universities to continue to take their annual escalator toward ever higher tuition are formidable. At public universities, the principal driver comes from the long-term withdrawal of state funds. At private institutions, rapidly rising costs are propelled by continuously swelling student services and ballooning nonacademic bureaucracies.

Still, colleges that have devoted imagination and commitment show that even with the financial stranglehold in which most schools are locked, the spiral can actually be arrested. College leaders need to recognize that prices have shot up too far. In the next budget cycle, as they face their treacherous spreadsheets—and before they add yet another percentage point to next year's tuition—they must act to roll back the perilous climb.

Of course, severe financial damage inflicted by the coronavirus crisis will toss out most of higher education's previous economic calculations. College and universities have entered a new era of even sharper enrollment declines, causing schools to be faced with unforeseen and damaging consequences.

SMALL COLLEGES

In the wake of a recent series of small college closings, the takeaway for small private institutions is that their days may be numbered. Since these schools are largely dependent on student tuition in a time when demographic changes mean fewer available high school graduates, they might as well be on an endangered-species list.

To staunch the bleeding, many small colleges have cut things to the bone or, alternatively, invested in country-club style improvements to appeal to students and their families—strategies that may have saved some. But this may only delay the impact of relentless market forces. Some observers aren't as pessimistic, it should be said.

"We continue to believe—and we think we've documented it pretty well—that most small colleges have the capability to be resilient in the face of these challenges," said Richard Ekman, president of the Council of Independent Colleges, in *Inside Higher Ed* (Seltzer, 2017b). "There are a small number of colleges that are in very serious trouble," he said. "But there are also a significant number of small colleges, twenty percent of them, that are just soaring. They're doing very well."

But Moody's predicts that the number of small failing colleges and universities will triple in the coming years and mergers will double (Woodhouse, 2015). One strategy for these colleges to avoid extinction is to diversify—to avoid a precarious reliance on residential students. And one way to do that is by adding online programs to the mix.

The challenge for many small colleges is that they see online courses as at odds with their very identity. After all, these institutions embrace intimacy as central to their mission, with close, mentoring relationships between faculty and students, and deep, comradely connections among students—essential ingredients of highly engaged learning. For many, online fails to meet these crucial educational ambitions. Instead, they reject virtual instruction as alienated learning, with isolated faculty and students coldly facing inert computer screens—not one another.

Yet in post-industrial America, the digital world is as "real" as it gets, with most of us doing our shopping, binge-watching our favorite shows, texting and chatting with friends and following them on Facebook, clacking away at keyboards all day at work, and Zooming online with co-workers in the pandemic. Today, serious research is impossible without searching databases, hunting references on Google Scholar, and emailing colleagues worldwide. Rejecting online is a retreat into nostalgia.

One problem is that some faculty long for a return to the simpler times of the past. Small schools—mostly in the Northeast and Midwest—are charming stage sets of Jeffersonian pastoral democracy, a fantasy even in its own time.

That's one reason why so few small colleges have jumped into providing online programs. "About fifty percent of U.S. colleges and universities have no more than a smattering of online enrollments, with little, if any, offered by most small private schools," said Babson's Jeffrey Seaman.

There is growing recognition of the quality of online models. With the scholarly literature almost universally confirming that online may be as good or better than conventional instruction, arguments against it seem a bit curmudgeonly, following those who turn their backs on solid evidence.

It turns out that online programs open education to those who can't attend otherwise. Nontraditional students now comprise nearly three-quarters of America's college population (Ross-Gordon, 2011). With many young adults working, caring for families, or traveling on the job, commuting to campus is not so easy and may even present real hardship, an impossible burden when you're occupied with sometimes crushing demands at home or at work. As small colleges reach out to these new students, they might also turn threadbare balance sheets from red to black.

Small colleges have a good chance at turning things around and thriving if they give online a chance and recruit older, mid-career students. Chances are your online students will be honored to "walk," diploma in hand, finally visiting your beautiful campus at commencement.

ONLINE COSTS

In a study comparing online with face-to-face courses, the online learning group WCET concluded that virtual courses are more expensive than those delivered on campus. If you focus on the report's narrow results, based merely on course tuition and fees, as well as selected instructional elements, you're sure to be led astray. I've seen perplexing media stories that inflate the report's puzzling findings: "Online Education Costs More, Not Less," declared a headline in a leading story in *Inside Higher Ed* (Straumsheim, 2017).

The study found that digital courses are not only more costly to produce than on-campus classes, but on the whole, after adding fees, online tuition is greater, too. While the results may be technically accurate, based on the limited terms set by the study's investigators, its broader analysis is seriously flawed.

As an on-campus student, to get to your class each morning, you either drive from your apartment and park your car at the nearest college lot, or you roll out of your dorm room and stroll across campus. After showing your ID to a security guard, you might stop off at the cafeteria for coffee and a bagel. After class, you may wander over to the campus gym to work out. None of the costs of these common university services outside of the classroom—parking, dormitory, grounds maintenance, security, cafeteria, and fitness center—were calculated in WCET's research, nor are any of them available to remote learners.

And while it appears to make perfect sense, when comparing online with on-campus teaching, to identify elements of instruction only—such as faculty compensation, instructional design and learning materials, among nearly two dozen other items selected for review in the WCET study—to appreciate the crucial distinctions, what was ignored may be more decisive than what the study counted as essential.

In his widely read blog, consultant Tony Bates was quick to puncture the report's methods and conclusions, commenting that it "confused rather than clarified the discussion about costs and price" (Bates, 2017). Troubled by its research bias, Bates observed that most elements under review in the study covered distance education, while routine expenses running face-to-face classes, especially substantial "sunk" costs, like buildings and parking, were largely missing.

Even the budget for academic information technology was excluded, while software that manages learning management systems, naturally found its way in. An institution's LMS—used equally by residential as well as remote students—represents merely a fraction of the substantial sums invested in information technology more generally. Excluded, too, are more common-place costs of face-to-face education—air-conditioning in the summer, heat in winter, cleaning services all year long—costs conventionally lumped into "overhead," expenses that fully apply on campus, but not one penny of which supports remote learners. Compared to the vast sums required to house an on-campus population, the costs of virtual instruction are trivial.

The WCET team dug meticulously into the data it collected, but it failed to ask all the right questions, nor did it look over the classroom walls to uncover meaningful clues elsewhere on campus. Residential students don't attend classes in isolated nodes in undifferentiated space. They enter their face-to-face courses as part of a rich complex of academic, social, and learner services that, together, constitute the modern campus. To isolate the face-to-face classroom from the total on-campus student experience makes little sense. Today, the cost of running a substantial university, largely to accommodate residential students, often runs into tens of millions of dollars per year. A tiny fraction of these costs supports remote student instruction.

Looking at on-campus tuition from a student's perspective, in a far more incisive way than the study, families soon discover that it does not include air fare or gas to travel to and from campus, nor tolls or other travel expenses

72 Scaling-up

to get to college, say, four or five times a year. Nor does it include student accommodation and meals. The College Board says that, on average, families must add about $10,000 a year to cover room and board.

In a virtual course, however, even if you're hit with a modest technology fee tacked on to online tuition, that's it. There are no surprises—no extra travel costs or room and board to cover. Yet WCET's in-depth survey, with responses from 197 senior college and university officials, concludes that tuition for digital courses is greater than on-campus prices, leaving us with the false impression that the total cost to earn a digital degree is more expensive than face-to-face education.

Calculated from inside a family's budget, going online is hands-down far less expensive than face-to-face instruction. Compared with their on-campus peers, students taking virtual classes save many thousands of dollars a year. To appreciate the difference in price between digital and face-to-face education, it's misleading to look at what students pay for individual courses only—a curiously institutionally centric exercise. It's far more revealing, as well as decidedly more practical, to calculate what families can afford, based on a thorough account of *everything* that goes into earning a degree, not on what counts in tallying a university classroom balance sheet.

The knockout blow to the belief that online is more expensive than residential instruction comes from this thought experiment: your college is faced with enrolling, say, a thousand new students. To accommodate the unexpected increase in your on-campus population, massive new facilities will be needed—new academic buildings, lecture halls, laboratories and, of course, classrooms—requiring millions of dollars in unbudgeted charges. If your institution is like others in the U.S., chances are your trustees and senior officers will face a crisis, concluding that your college cannot afford to enroll them, forcing your eager new freshmen to apply elsewhere. In an illuminating alternative, however, enrolling a thousand new students online will be nothing like what is required on campus. More faculty, of course, and an additional cadre of instructional designers, but not much more. Your thousand new students will be very welcome online.

JOINED AT THE HIP?

Despite my argument that online and in-person constitute separate campuses, nonetheless, they have been joined at the hip for years. Consider that at most schools, every course—whether online or on campus—must now post syllabi on a class website. Both virtual and residential students now log onto the same school-wide learning management system. At many colleges, homework assignments, readings, watching videos, and taking tests are commonly done online.

Flipped classrooms and HyFlex (see Chapter 13) instruction depend on digital instruction for at least half of each semester and, increasingly, MOOCs have been introduced as part of many college curricula. Not as common, but surely soon to infiltrate many classes, social media websites often serve as pedagogical illustrations, online and on campus.

In some classes, faculty teach face-to-face on campus while simultaneously streaming their lectures to other students, either located in a classroom at a remote site or accessing video versions of the course on laptops or smartphones worldwide. Some discover that virtual teaching can act like a training camp, where instructors acquire innovative pedagogical methods that they exploit in residential classes. As digital education enters the academic mainstream, some instructors offer courses in conventional classrooms to on-campus students and deliver the same class in virtual space to remote learners at the same university during the same semester.

Today, both digital and residential students can manipulate the same software remotely as do scientists, engineers, and scholars. Accessing large-scale systems at a distance is now possible in many industries, with virtual and in-person students performing experiments or running operations remotely with equal confidence and facility as those at the site.

Several years ago, at NYU, a state accrediting team was uneasy about approving an online electrical engineering master's degree program because they worried about student access to a virtual lab, a requirement that seemed pretty risky to them. Eventually, the degree was approved when reviewers recognized that students could perform experiments digitally, just as they might play a video game, by touching a screen and tapping on a keyboard. Ironically, students in the residential section of the program had been running the same virtual lab in their on-campus class for years.

At many schools, NYU for one, students are free to mix and match, taking some of their classes on campus and others online. Andy DiPaolo, executive director emeritus of Stanford University's Center for Professional Development, told me, "We never made a distinction between online and on campus. Your degree doesn't say you earned it online. Students have the option of going online or on campus or taking a blended degree. It's a Stanford degree."

It's highly unlikely that a residential freshman, entering one of the nation's colleges will earn a degree without being plugged-in virtually, even after the pandemic. The student might take at least one—if not several—online classes, perhaps participate in a flipped classroom (or two), enroll in a

74   Scaling-up

MOOC, and possibly access a remote lab. During the student's time in college, there will surely be other routine digital practices, supported by the school's LMS and other academic software.

When history books are written about the debates between online and face-to-face, readers will wonder what all the fuss was about and why there was so much mischief. Looking back on the fierce battles between movies and television in the nineteen-fifties, when Hollywood worried that tv would put it out of business, it's uncanny how today, the two have blended so closely that they have swallowed each other whole. Most of us can't possibly imagine giving up one for the other. Chances are, someday, the online versus on campus dichotomy will be equally incomprehensible.

If you search Google Scholar for "comparing online with on-campus instruction," you'll be astonished to discover that there are more than 42,000 entries. When digital education was introduced more than two decades ago, after thousands of studies, slicing and dicing research in dozens of ways, results consistently showed that there was no significant difference between the two modes.

Peter Shea, associate provost for online learning at the University of Albany, points out that there is still tough work ahead, despite the fact that *on average* there is no significant difference between the two modes. Shea cautioned, "Just as many studies find online learning to be as good as they find it to be worse than face-to-face education." The real question is to tease out what features of virtual instruction will show consistently better outcomes.

CRITICAL MASS

As a longtime official in online-education programs, the puzzling question to me is why, after more than two decades, does online represent merely a third of college enrollment? Why doesn't it occupy a greater share of the market? By comparison, for example, learning management systems captured more than ninety percent of universities years ago.

One reason is that digital education at U.S. colleges and universities suffers from a legacy of suspicion that has made wider adoption challenging. "Online education has a troubled past," recalled Phil Hill at MindWires. "In the early days, schools just dumped things online, thinking they'd get rich quick. To move ahead, online has to get over its sour reputation."

Much of that poor history comes from for-profit providers, since they were among the first to go online in a big way, attracting wads of Wall

Street cash that let them quickly expand to enroll millions of students. Disastrously, as it turned out, with notoriously poor outcomes and piles of student debt. Looking over the campus gates at for-profits, faculty at public and private institutions shuddered at what they saw (see Chapter 11).

It is highly unlikely that virtual education will ever achieve total saturation in the academic market. Good chunks of it will never go online (and probably shouldn't). Many small, liberal arts colleges, as we've seen, representing about ten to fifteen percent of higher ed, say they couldn't be less interested; digital education does not fulfill their mission.

"At small, private institutions, it's not just what happens in class that matters," remarked Babson's Jeff Seaman. "What happens on campus—football games, fraternities, partying—often matters most."

Seaman predicts that even when it achieves its greatest share, online will never reach a hundred percent, but will plateau at about fifty percent.

Eric Fredericksen, associate vice president for online learning at the University of Rochester, disagrees, claiming that since digital education is not one thing, but a "continuum," stretching from face-to-face to completely online, it will extend way beyond fifty percent.

"I'm totally impressed by thirty percent," he says, noting that digital learning and teaching options have invaded nearly every university classroom—on campus, online, and blended. Optimistic about the future of virtual education, Fredericksen argues that "online is a catalyst for academic transformation."

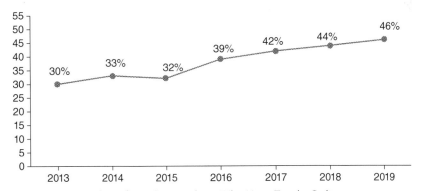

FIGURE 5.4 Number of Faculty Members Who Have Taught Online
Source: Inside Higher Ed/Gallup (see www.insidehighered.com/news/survey/professors-slow-steady-acceptance-online-learning-survey)

76 Scaling-up

Unlike an LMS, online learning is not a piece of plug-in software or a digital device you can carry in your pocket. Not a gadget that opens your garage door, digital education depends only partly on technology. In fact, virtual education is not a technology at all, but an umbrella term characterizing a wide variety of technology-enabled pedagogies, only some delivered to students off campus.

In his diffusion of innovation theory, the late American sociologist Everett Rogers explored the rate at which new ideas and technologies spread (Rogers, 2003). He found that an innovation must be widely adopted to be sustainable. As a new idea becomes accepted, there is a point at which it reaches critical mass, enlisting a sufficient number of adherents so that it generates continued, sustained growth.

Among the most striking pieces of data released recently show that the number of faculty teaching online at the nation's colleges and universities has steadily—and quite surprisingly—increased in the last decade to what appears to be a pivotal point. As an *Inside Higher Ed* Gallup survey's results show in the following figure, nearly fifty percent of American college faculty have taught online, a dramatic leap beyond thirty percent just seven years earlier (Jaschik et al., 2019). The survey was conducted a few years before the COVID-19 pandemic invaded the nation's campuses. Of course, in the academic emergency, nearly all the country's faculty were drafted online (see Chapter 1).

It took almost a quarter of a century for digital instruction to be adopted by a third of the higher-education market. While its growth was often hobbled by rough speed bumps along the way, given the current accelerated rate of adoption by almost half of the country's faculty, digital education may have already achieved critical mass.

REFERENCES

American Association of University Professors. (2018, October). *Background Facts on Contingent Faculty Positions*. Retrieved June 1, 2020, from www.aaup.org/issues/contingency/background-facts

American Council on Education (2019). *Race and Ethnicity in Higher Education*.

Bates, T. (2017, February 20). *What Counts When You Cost Online Learning?* Online Learning and Distance Education Resources. Retrieved from www.tonybates.ca/2017/02/20/what-counts-when-you-cost-online-learning/

Berman, J. (2015, March 28). Why More US Colleges Will Go Under in the Next Few Years. *MarketWatch*.

Berman, J. (2018, November 19). Here's What It Will Take to Make College Tuition-Free. *MarketWatch*.

Branbery, S. (2015, December 23). Higher Education Marketing Trends. *LinkedIn Pulse*. Retrieved June 1, 2020.

Candid. (2017, October 6). University of Hawaii Receives $117 Million Commitment. *Candid*. Retrieved June 3, 2020, from http://philanthropynewsdigest.org/news/university-of-hawai-i-receives-117-million-commitment

Christensen, C. and J. Eyring. (2011). *The Innovative University*. San Francisco: Jossey-Bass.

Crow, M. (2017, November 15). Personal communication (R. Ubell, Interviewer).

Edmit. (2020). College Financial Health. *Edmit*. Retrieved May 30, 2020, from https://edmit.me/browse/

Education Dive. (2020, September 17). A Look at Trends in College Consolidation Since 2016. *Education Dive*.

Griffen, T. (2016, July 29). A Dozen Things I've Learned from Andy Grove About Business and Strategy. *25IQ*.

Horn, M. (2015, April 23). Report That Says Online Learning Growth Is Slowing Misses Big Picture. *Forbes*.

Hussar, B. (2020). The Condition of Education 2020. *National Center for Education Statistics*.

Jaschik, Scott. (2015, November 15). The Missing Low-Income Students. *Inside Higher Ed*.

Jaschik, Scott. (2019, May 28). Illinois Will End Residential MBA, *Inside Higher Ed*.

Jaschik, Scott et al. (2019). 2019 Survey of Faculty Attitudes on Technology. *Inside Higher Ed*.

Johnson, G. M. (2019). On-Campus and Fully-Online University Students: Comparing Demographics, Digital Technology and Learning Characteristics. *Journal of University Teaching and Learning Practice (JUTLF)*, 12(1).

Karr, J. (2017, November 3). Saying Farewell to Education Life. *New York Times*.

Kezar, A. and D. Maxey. (2013, May–June). *The Changing Academic Workforce*. Washington, DC: Association of Governing Boards of Universities and Colleges.

Kim, J. and E. Maloney. (2020). *Learning and the Future of Higher Education*. Baltimore: Johns Hopkins University Press.

King, A. and B. Baatartogtkh. (2015, Fall). How Useful Is the Theory of Disruptive Innovation? *MIT Sloan Management Review*, 57.

Krupnick, M. (2018, August 30). Bending the Law of Supply and Demand, Some Colleges Are Dropping Their Prices. *The Hechinger Report*. Retrieved from https://online.champlain.edu/blog/some-colleges-are-dropping-prices

Lapore, J. (2014, June 23). The Disruptive Machine. *New Yorker*.

Learning House. (2019). Online Learning College Students 2019. *Learning House*. Retrieved from www.learninghouse.com/web-ocs2019-infographic/

Lederman, D. (2018, November 7). Online Education Ascends. *Inside Higher Ed*.

Lieberman, M. (2018, July 11). A College Prices Its Online Program at 60% Less. *Inside Higher Ed*.

Lyotard, J. F. (1984). *The Postmodern Condition*. Minneapolis: University of Minnesota Press.

McGuire, M. A. (2012). Subprime Education: For-Profit Colleges and the Problem with Title IV Student Aid. *Duke Law Journal*, 119–160.

78 Scaling-up

McKenzie, L. (2018, September 19). An Elite Online Bachelor's Degree. *Inside Higher Ed*.

Moody's Investment Service. (2019, December 10). Outlook for U.S. Higher Education Sector Changed to Stable from Negative on Steady Revenue Gains. *Moody's Investor Service*. Retrieved from https://www.moodys.com/research/Moodys-Outlook-for-US-higher-education-sector-changed-to-stable-PBM_1207036

Moody's Investment Service. (2020, April 7). *COVID-19 Puts Pressure on Higher Education Finances*. Retrieved from https://www.moodys.com/research/Moodys-Covid-19-puts-pressure-on-higher-education-finances-PBC_1222963

National Student Clearinghouse. (2017). *Research Center*. National Student Clearinghouse. Retrieved June 1, 2020, from https://nscresearchcenter.org/report

Perry, S. (2013, June 17). The Stubborn 2% Giving Rate. *The Chronicle of Philanthropy*.

Pew Charitable Trusts. (2009). *Two Decades of Federal and State Education Funding*. Issue Brief. Pew Charitable Trusts. Retrieved from https://www.pewtrusts.org/en/research-and-analysis/issue-briefs/2019/10/two-decades-of-change-in-federal-and-state-higher-education-funding

Piketty, T. (2014). *Capital in the Twenty-First Century*. Cambridge, MA: Harvard University Press.

Pitsker, K. (2015, October). 10 Colleges Actually Lower the Cost of Tuition. *Kiplinger*.

Rawls, T. (2020, June 1). Achieving Economies of Scale in Higher Education. *Evolllution*. Retrieved June 1, 2020, from https://evolllution.com/managing-institution/higher_ed_business/achieving-economies-of-scale-in-higher-education/

Rogers, E. M. (2003). *Diffusion of Innovations*. New York: Simon & Schuster.

Ross-Gordon, J. (2011, Winter). Research on Adult Learners: Supporting the Needs of a Student Population That Is No Longer Nontraditional. *Association of American Colleges and Universities*, 13(1).

Schanzer, O. (2020, July 2020). *Professor Precarious: Adjuncts in the Time of COVID*. Economic Hardship Reporting Project. Retrieved from https://economichardship.org/2020/07/professor-precarious-adjunct-professors-covid-19/

Scutari, M. (2018, September 10). Sharing Their Treasure: More Evidence That Only Donors Can Prevent Tuition Hikes. *Inside Philanthropy*.

Seaman, J. et al. (2018). *Grade Increase: Tracking Distance Learning in the United States*. Babson Survey Group. Retrieved from https://www.bayviewanalytics.com/reports/gradeincrease.pdf

Seltzer, R. (2017a, September 25). The Tuition Reset Strategy. *Inside Higher Ed*.

Seltzer, R. (2017b, November 13). Days of Reckoning. *Inside Higher Ed*.

Seltzer, R. (2018, August 17). Antidote to Med Student Debt. *Inside Higher Ed*.

Shah, D. (2019, December 2). By the Numbers: MOOCs in 2019. *Class Central*. Retrieved from www.classcentral.com/report/mooc-stats-2019/

Sloan Foundation. (2009). *Anytime, Anyplace Learning*. Retrieved May 27, 2020, from https://sloan.org/programs/completed-programs/anytime-anyplace-learning

Statista. (2020). College Enrollment in the United States from 1965 to 2018 and Projections up to 2029 for Public and Private Colleges. *Statista*. Retrieved June 1, 2020, from www.statista.com/statistics/183995/us-college-enrollment-and-projections-in-public-and-private-institutions/

Straumsheim, C. (2017, February 17). Online Ed Costs More, Not Less. *Inside Higher Ed*.

Thys, F. (2020, May 8). One Third of Private, 4-Year Colleges Are at High Risk Financially, Model Predicts. *WBUR*. Retrieved May 30, 2020, from www.wbur.org/edify/2020/05/08/higher-education-financial-crisis

Ubell, R. (2009, December 22). Dewey Goes Online. *Educause Review*.

Ubell, R. (2017, January 23). Can MOOCs Cure the Tuition Epidemic? *IEEE Spectrum*.

U.S. Bureau of Labor Statistics. (2020, June 3). *College Tuition and Fees*. Retrieved from https://data.bls.gov/timeseries/CUUR0000SEEB01?output_view=pct_12mths

Valbrun, M. (2018, September 13). Bucking the 'Prestige Pricing' Trend. *Inside Higher Ed*.

Valbrun, M. (2019, May 10). Discount Rates Hit Record Highs. *Inside Higher Ed*.

Woodhouse, K. (2015, September 28). Closures to Triple. *Inside Higher Ed*.

Zinshteyn, M. (2016, December 6). Colleges Face New Reality as Number of High School Graduates Will Decline. *The Hechinger Report*. Retrieved from https://hechingerreport.org/colleges-face-new-reality-number-high-schools-graduates-will-decline/

6

Outsourcing vs. Insourcing

As college leaders scroll through their perilous spreadsheets, anxiously looking for the most productive way to spend their meager resources, this may be the right time for them to rethink their usual approach—and aggressively invest in online education. After all, with national on-campus enrollments faltering, online numbers continue to speed forward.

Informed projections say that American universities have already run out of enough eighteen-year-olds to fill the millions of freshmen empty seats in their classrooms (Grawe, 2018). Those demographic realities have already forced dozens of colleges to go under (Education Dive, 2020). If colleges continue to follow the usual practice of routinely adding or subtracting a few dollars from existing programs, rather than moving into new markets, their schools may soon be at risk.

These crucial economic facts have been known for years. So why haven't otherwise thoughtful senior academic officers absorbed these lessons, adopting virtual instruction to lift higher education out of its deepening financial hole?

Reluctance to go online is often influenced by a major sabotaging myth— that digital instruction is far too expensive for most colleges, with media stories citing the high cost of putting even a single class online. One article reported that Udacity, a company that creates large-scale online courses, budgeted $200,000 per course, while edX, a joint Harvard-MIT effort,

80

charged $250,000 for its design and consulting services. *Forbes* noted that the giant online program management (OPM) company called 2U invested $5 to $10 million in software and marketing to launch an online MBA at the University of North Carolina (Gana, 2018).

With reports citing such whopping numbers to go online, it's no wonder some senior academic officers are cowed. So, let's take a look a little more calmly at how to go online without going bust.

ORGANIC GROWTH

At Stevens Institute of Technology, a prescient benefactor thought it might be a good idea to experiment with a $350,000 investment to launch a couple of online master's degrees. That was back in 1999. Today, that modest seed money has bloomed online into eighteen master's and fifty graduate certificates, representing three thousand online and blended enrollments today, over time, generating millions in digital tuition revenue.

Starting off cautiously, following Stevens, any college can introduce digital programs step-by-step, building virtual degrees by corralling a few daring faculty members to work together with a couple of new hires—especially an experienced instructional designer (see Chapter 2). Most colleges already have learning management software installed for their on-campus students, technical infrastructure that can easily serve as the digital heart of a virtual campus.

Colleges don't need to launch their first online degrees all at once. Tactically, it's wise to build only the one or two needed for the first semester. Tuition generated from initial courses is likely to subsidize the next ones. And so on. By the time a college is ready to launch its next round of online degrees, funds from those delivered in the opening semesters will help drive the next few.

At Stevens, self-financing, organic growth allowed us to continue over the life of our online programs, without ever resorting to outside investment again, drawing exclusively on online revenue from delivering digital courses semester after semester. I took the same approach when I moved to NYU and it worked there, too.

John Vivolo, director of Online Education at the Katz School of Science and Health at Yeshiva University, dismisses inflated online development costs feared by many college leaders (Vivolo, 2019). "A full program, say, of six courses, should cost $150,000 to $200,000," Vivolo said. For a number of years, I worked alongside Vivolo at the NYU Engineering School's virtual education unit, Tandon Online.

82 Scaling-up

Of course, many say that the biggest cost is not building programs but getting the word out with marketing efforts. This, too, can be done with a college's existing staff, argues Vivolo. Rather than building a costly digital recruitment and marketing team from scratch, new online programs can partner with university promotion departments, sharing expertise and budgets.

"Often, the problem is not money," Vivolo claimed, "but stubborn academic bureaucratic intransigence that prevents residential marketing staff from supporting new digital programs. If you treat online and on-campus equally, your recruitment investment can easily be piggybacked."

In another cost-saving move, Vivolo encouraged new online units to enlist student support in video recording and editing online courses, among other technical crafts. "Accept that your courses may not be perfect at first, but by exploiting rapid prototyping, they'll get better and better every year," Vivolo reassured. "Starting off, you needn't run super interactive courses. Some video and a few PowerPoints should do the trick."

My own experience at The New School, where I led an online certificate in 2019, is instructive. This generation of online student support workers can be remarkably intuitive about mastering digital techniques, often helping to produce surprisingly high-quality online courses at low cost. At a recording session for an online course I delivered, I was struck by student professional command of the medium (see Chapter 2).

Chances are, right now, your CFO and other top academic leaders may be considering upgrading the college gym or installing a new vegan station in the cafeteria, or buffing-up a giant lecture hall with whiz-bang projection equipment. None of these attractive improvements will add a single tuition dollar to the bottom line. It's far more prudent to shift whatever cash a college can earmark from neutral or even negative tuition-generating investments and convert it into digital currency, attracting an entirely new stream of online revenue. Of course, there is no guarantee that by introducing virtual instruction your college will hit it out of the park; but by avoiding it, there is a good chance you'll strike out.

Charles Darwin, teleported from nineteenth-century Cambridge, could enter any classroom at Harvard today and, without the least hesitation, stride directly to the lectern and deliver his lecture on evolution as if not a thing had changed in a hundred and fifty years. (To keep up with the times, however, Darwin would need to learn how to display images of his finches on PowerPoint slides.)

But a professor who retired twenty years ago, clicking open her laptop, would find digital education nearly unrecognizable. In just a couple of decades, MOOCs, flipped classrooms, video streaming, digital exercises, remote labs, and other developments have transformed online instruction with new technologies and innovative pedagogies. Bewildered about how to respond to market forces compelling them to move online, most universities and college leaders are mystified as to how to proceed.

To move ahead online, most senior college faculty and administrators must make decisions for which they are largely unprepared. With sufficient resources, they're fairly comfortable going over blueprints with starchitects to erect new glass-and-steel academic towers, but when it comes to virtual education, most are as befuddled as Fred MacMurray in the classic Disney movie, *The Absent-Minded Professor.*

Commonly elevated to academic leadership at a time before the internet invaded, few senior faculty members have taken an online class, let alone taught one. In an essay in *Inside Higher Ed*, I noted that data showed that "older and higher-ranking faculty members exhibit the least support for online education" (Ubell, 2016). It's no wonder that schools, squeezed by shrinking budgets, often leave online learning on the cutting-room floor.

Over the last couple of decades since online learning was first introduced, universities have invested hundreds of millions in campus facilities—laboratories, maker spaces, football stadiums, and so on. In contrast, while online learning (both in revenues and students) was expanding at double-digit growth and with the residential population flattening or declining, only a few schools recognized the strategic retreat of investing in the past as higher education starved its future.

Years ago, Harvard Business School, among others, accurately predicted that we were headed for a totally immersive digital economy, cautioning industry that it would enter a life-and-death struggle unless institutions accommodated themselves to new digital facts.

"The digitization of the economy is one of the most critical issues of our time, proclaimed *Harvard Business Review* (Anderson, 2016). "Digital technologies are rapidly transforming both business practices and societies, and they are integral to the innovation-driven economies of the future." Curiously, most academic leaders paid no attention to business school wisdom, imagining somehow that higher education would be given a pass.

Worried about conservative faculty pushback and fearing the damage to their reputations if they delivered what many academics considered an inferior product, many schools backed away from entering the online market. I participated in interminably tedious deliberations over digital education as years slipped by while senior faculty and administrators scratched their

84 Scaling-up

eggheads and dithered, issuing grandiose reports on an online utopia yet to come.

Pretending to support online learning, some schools invested in "technology-enhanced" education, a sprinkling of digital gadgets around campus, mainly for residential students. In consequence, schools left a wide-open gap in the campus gates for OPMs to waltz in. Taking a lesson from Darwin's Galápagos birds, OPMs occupied a rich commercial niche, feasting on swelling virtual enrollments as many in higher education sniffed at digital growth.

ONLINE PROGRAM MANAGEMENT

Schools that depend largely on tuition for their financial stability find themselves in a tight spot. Under stress, institutions are looking for alternative revenue streams. With the online national upward curve looking more like a smile than a frown, digital education might be a good bet.

More colleges are looking to online programs for financial health these days—and even survival—as demographic changes are leading fewer students to seek traditional campus experiences. But as many academic leaders look around for help going online, they often can't find experts at their own institutions with the experience and skills to build a virtual campus, or to run the sophisticated marketing efforts it takes to attract students around the country and around the world. That's why OPMs—online program managers, commercial vendors with expertise in launching and delivering digital programs—eagerly bounded in.

According to a survey conducted in 2020, a quarter of online learning leaders said their institutions employed an OPM, up from twelve percent in 2017, with student marketing and recruitment as the most common support provided. About half used online program management for virtual course and program development (Lederman, 2020).

In financial circles, OPM refers to "other people's money," but while OPM in higher education clearly means something else, one of the big attractions for universities from the $3 billion marketplace (Holon IQ, 2019) is that OPMs in education—in addition to providing instructional design, student support, market research, course design, retention programs, recruitment, and advanced digital techniques—can also act as investment firms, financing virtual programs for colleges and universities in exchange for a big bite of tuition revenue.

Rather than waiting to generate organic growth by going it alone, colleges can move faster into the online world by turning to one of dozens of vendors out there that help schools build programs (Hill, 2019). Among these are full-service OPMs that will not only act as an investment bank, but also perform course-building functions as well as conduct global digital recruitment. By contrast, fee-for-service vendors offer an à la carte menu, delivering a range of technical, pedagogical, and recruitment services, allowing a college to manage part of the effort, while the vendor does the rest.

With colleges under severe budget stress and some eager to go online quickly to wriggle out of their economic straight jackets, it's no wonder they are seduced by OPMs, not only for their skills in launching and marketing new academic programs, but even more crucially, for their enticing overtures to finance institutions taking their first steps into the virtual world.

In exchange for financing new online programs and conjuring virtual magic for online academic programs—building infrastructure, global digital marketing, and financial investment—most full-service OPMs commonly take about half of resulting online tuition revenue, more or less splitting the take. Typical contracts call for colleges to share 45 to 65 percent of tuition revenue. In financing online launches, OPMs assume the risk of fronting course development and recruitment for a year or more before any tuition revenue is realized. As more vendors enter the market and as the number of deals multiply, some agreements have shifted to hybrid formulas, incorporating fee-for-service options or a guaranteed fixed-fee, coupled with a more modest revenue share (Hill, 2020).

"The revenue share is outrageous," comments NYU Steinhardt's Dominic Brewer, who partnered with 2U and HotChalk to launch several degrees (Brewer, 2017). "But, of course, we couldn't have done it ourselves."

Ilan Jacobsohn, former senior director of distributed education at The New School, says, "OPMs assume the risk. If your program fails, your school might look bad, but it's the OPM that loses the money."

As the OPM industry expands to meet demand among private and public institutions, new sectors have emerged to fill niche markets. Edtech observer Phil Hill of MindWires divides the industry into several domains, with the big vendors, Pearson, 2U, and Wiley, among others, offering mostly bundled services, while Noodle Partners, Extension Engine, and others deliver fee-for-service options (Hill, 2019).

MOOCs, with their immense learner audience, recently entered the OPM industry, providing colleges and universities with access to their combined one hundred and ten million learners as prospective students to enroll in MOOC-based joint degrees and certificates from Coursera, edX, Future Learn, and a handful of others (Class Central, 2019). Phil Hill notes that MOOC providers split revenue with colleges at about forty to fifty percent.

86 Scaling-up

Holon IQ, a market analytics company, identifies several other OPM categories, including "specialist," with Orbis Education and Apollidon among them, and "university," listing Kaplan, Bridgeport and several others. Holon IQ identifies 61 OPM vendors with more than 620 schools under contract—emerging as a crowded and highly competitive marketplace, scrambling for clients (Holon IQ, 2019).

While a handful of selective schools have ventured into digital education as part of their basic curricula, Harvard doesn't offer a single completely online degree. So why, with all its firepower—at $40.9 billion, Harvard's endowment is the richest in the world (Hess, 2019)—did Harvard turn to an OPM to help launch its online business data analytics certificate? The agreement calls for 2U, an OPM, remarkably valued at $2.027 billion (MarcoTrends, 2020), with top-brand university clients like Yale, NYU and Berkeley, to work jointly with Harvard faculty to make it happen.

"We don't have the resources to support a marketing effort of that magnitude nor provide individual user support of that intensity," claimed Peter Bol, Harvard's former vice provost for advances in learning (Bol, 2017). Bol admitted, in effect, that despite its cavernous deep pockets, Harvard was asleep at the virtual wheel while online learning was taking off across the nation. Commenting on the conundrum in *Inside Higher Ed*, AnnaLee Saxenian, dean of Berkeley's School of Information, observed, "Even universities with substantial endowments lack the technology and marketing expertise to bring high-quality online programs to scale" (Dimeo, 2017).

OPMs provide services that on-campus higher education has largely ignored, chief among them web-savvy marketing and recruitment. "For many traditional colleges starting online programs these days, the solution has been to outsource as much of the business operations as possible (including marketing and advertising) by using companies like 2U," reports senior editor Jeffrey R. Young in *EdSurge News* (Young, 2017).

"Universities have gone from the Pony Express to jet aircraft in one fell swoop," observed NYU's Brewer (Brewer, 2017). "Enrollment management is from the nineteenth century, with spreadsheets and file cabinets."

In addition to offering to finance new virtual degrees, OPMs also claim to exploit more sophisticated techniques in achieving greater enrollment than conventional marketing efforts at other institutions. Racing ahead with pricey, new digital recruitment methods, OPMs report sizeable gains over college-run online programs. In an Eduventures study of online growth from 2012 to 2016, OPMs generated significantly greater enrollments over other online programs, successfully generating forty percent undergraduate growth, leaving other virtual undergrad programs behind at about fifteen percent. Similarly, graduate OPMs outpaced others, rising to nearly twenty-five percent, compared with about fifteen percent for others (Garrett, 2018).

Meanwhile, OPMs emerge as villains, accused by The Century Foundation of fleecing university treasuries with hard-bitten terms and poor value for the money. Analyzing about seventy OPM contacts with colleges, the foundation reported, as expected, that most agreements split revenue fifty-fifty, with one turning over eighty percent of tuition revenue to the vendor (The Century Foundation, 2019). Troubled by lengthy contracts of five years or more, often with strict exiting rules, the foundation discovered that many agreements failed to protect student data from commercial sales. The report also disclosed that in some cases, OPMs even had a hand in devising curriculum, an unacceptable intrusion into academic affairs.

Not that OPMs are blameless, but the real offenders are skittish universities that failed to invest in their own digital future. Compared with business elite, academic leaders are thought of as far more sensible and risk averse, but their heads-in-the-sand virtual education policies turned out to be irresponsible. To pay for their inattention to the relentless digital economy—if they partner with OPMs—some universities must now split the take.

Thomas D'Aunno's experience is typical of those who go the OPM route. When D'Aunno, director of the Master of Health Administration and Health Policy & Management Programs at New York University's Robert F. Wagner Graduate School of Public Service, was hunting for the best way to launch a new online degree, he quickly discovered all the things he didn't know about the logistics of running an online program.

"The question was which OPM we were going to work with," he says, "not whether we were going to work with one." In its first semester, D'Aunno's new online master's not only reached its initial enrollment goal but things were going smoothly. Not incidentally, he's learned what it takes.

Into the next year, things weren't as rosy. Much of what was promised failed to materialize and D'Aunno parted company with his vendor. Today, internal staff has taken over. D'Aunno turned out to be an excellent student of what it takes.

A recent *Inside Higher Ed* faculty survey concluded that most professors and digital learning leaders generally oppose going outside to contract with OPMs to help deliver online academic programs, even though they are largely in favor of engaging them to market online programs to students (Lederman, 2019).

Since the pandemic, with enrollments declining, colleges are suffering from severe income declines, forcing many to either skip plans to introduce new online programs or turn to OPMs to build new digital income streams.

88   Scaling-up

"Folks are getting more and more comfortable understanding that they can't just offer a live Zoom on their learning management system and consider that high-quality online learning," said 2U CEO Chip Paucek (Schwartz, 2020). *Education Dive* reports that the OPM sector is booming with 85 colleges striking new deals in just the first half of 2020.

INSOURCING

On the other extreme, some institutions have decided to build their own virtual campuses without OPMs. Those include a handful of public and private institutions, including Southern New Hampshire University, Arizona State University, and the University of Central Florida, which have seen enrollments rise markedly, now surprisingly close to—or hitting—100,000 each (see Chapter 5).

First at Stevens and later at the NYU Tandon School of Engineering, we decided to do it ourselves, building an in-house unit, hiring experts in instructional design, digital recruitment, and other virtual crafts, enrolling thirty thousand online students in about twenty years at both Stevens and NYU. But with colleges all around us jumping into bed with OPMs, we wondered whether my colleagues and I at NYU were fooling ourselves. To explore whether we were making a mistake by continuing to go it alone, several years ago we invited three top OPMs to show us how each might help us launch a new online master's degree we had in mind.

Once proposals rolled in, we consulted the school's finance staff, who cautioned us against signing up, advising us that the economic benefits we were achieving on our own far outweighed anything we might gain from a partnership. The finance team reminded us that on our own, we pocketed it all. Without an OPM bankrolling us, luckily, we were able to back each online semester, drawn from our own online course revenue—even topping it off with a decent surplus.

While at first some universities may outsource online programs to help them jump digital hurdles, in the long run, many colleges that turn to OPMs, rather than build their own virtual units, may end up regretting their decision. Chances are, when online emerges as the best game in town, institutions lacking digital capabilities will be hamstrung, not knowing how to scale-up as remote learning becomes indispensable for the long-term health of higher education.

Outsourcing your institution's digital education infrastructure could impoverish your college, leaving it hollowed out and lacking in essential virtual competencies just when you will surely need them most. Partnering with an OPM is the equivalent of a patient with a serious illness popping pain killers rather than treating the underlying condition.

Of course, universities have outsourced a wide variety of tasks for years—think of food services and campus security as examples. But most of those functions are on the periphery of the university's mission, not at its very heart.

Sure, going online isn't cheap, but neither are science labs or football stadiums. Higher education has always found the money to support its scientists and athletes. Institutions with a clear vision find ways to finance infrastructure needed to fulfill their mission. Partnering with OPMs is an easy way out. The hard way is to go for what's best over the long haul.

For institutions that have already signed on with commercial vendors, it may be best just to go on blithely as a temporary measure, rolling in a Trojan horse, disguising your game plan to learn all you can about how they do it, hoping eventually to mirror their skills when you're finally on your own. Partnerships can be exploited by colleges as workshops to gain know-how, especially how to build active-learning courses or how to run a call center, among other competencies, like online staffing and budgeting. Once you get the hang of it, you're ready to take off your training wheels.

For most colleges and universities, perhaps the biggest challenge is how to recruit virtual learners with sophisticated, web-savvy techniques that may require—at the most elaborate end—fairly advanced knowledge of machine learning and other top-of-the-line tools, especially in selecting targeted databases and bidding on ad space in search engines, which are the costliest parts of going online.

In other words, partnering with OPMs may not be a bad idea if your plan essentially is to hire the company as your college's teacher, showing you how to operate in the space so you can eventually go it alone. But be careful. Make sure your agreement calls for you to own all the data your vendor collected on your behalf—especially recruitment and student information—so that you're not left holding an empty digital bag. But also remember that commonly, OPM contracts run for a fairly long stretch, some for as many as seven to ten years. So, if you're thinking of keeping your learning curve fairly short—think again.

Admittedly, virtual capabilities are not easy to come by, especially for institutions that have little or no experience. But historically, universities have not backed away from assuming a powerful role in what at first appeared to be overwhelming odds. On the contrary, over time, higher education has risen to overcome some of society's most intractable challenges. In the twentieth century, universities have conquered polio and diphtheria,

90 Scaling-up

among other traumatic diseases. Putting their best minds to it, there's little doubt that higher education can learn how to manage digital recruitment expertly too.

Then, too, some vendors have unbundled their services, so if you find that your college is prepared to hire its own cadre of instructional designers, for example, to work together with faculty members to produce virtual courses, but your institution is not up for managing digital recruitment, you might find it convenient to outsource just the marketing part of the job while performing other activities in house.

OPMs may be an expedient solution if your institution has only one or two online degree programs in mind. Until recently, most vendors have been brought in to run merely one—or just a handful—of programs, rarely managing the full curriculum, with dozens, if not thousands, of online courses. Partnering with an OPM is a quick way of jumping in without having to install a full-blown unit to handle it all like we did at NYU Tandon Online.

But if your institution is sensible, accepting that online learning will be a long-term university objective, then it's wise to perform a risk analysis, comparing the benefits and dangers of dealing with an outside vendor versus going solo.

In his widely followed blog, Joshua Kim, director of digital learning initiatives at the Dartmouth Center for the Advancement of Learning, insightfully remarked,

> What we really care about is the long-term resilience of our institutions, and our ability to meet our strategic goals and to support our larger institutional missions. Online education is integral to how education is changing. Online programs provide opportunities to not only bring in new (much needed) dollars, but also to build new institutional capacities.
>
> (Kim, 2018)

This chapter is not an argument against commercial vendors as corporate interlopers in academic space nor is it opposed to their unorthodox contractual terms. As a matter of fact, from all reports, on the whole, top OPMs are really good at it. Most colleges are pleased with the results, even while admitting that not all marriages are happy, with a few ending up so miserable, they get divorced. A few years ago, I visited an OPM facility of a first-rank firm and was quite impressed with its knowledgeable, sophisticated personnel and practices.

The way forward is to acknowledge that online no longer runs along academic side streets, but now occupies the main road. To succeed, higher education leaders must get some digital skin in the game and make big investments in home-grown virtual skills and infrastructure, building digital capacity to ensure the long-term viability of the university. At stake is not just the health of online learning, but the life of higher education itself.

REFERENCES

Anderson, L. (2016, March 24). The 4 Ways It Takes to Succeed in the Digital Economy. *Harvard Business Review*.

Bol, P. (2017, October 4). *Vice Provost, Advances in Learning*. Retrieved June 22, 2020, from www.macrotrends.net/stocks/charts/TWOU/2u/market-cap

Brewer, D. (2017, October 4). Dean Emeritus, NYU Steinhardt School (R. Ubell, Interviewer).

Century Foundation. (2019, September 13). *TCF Analysis of 70+ University-OPM Contracts Reveals Increasing Risks to Students, Public Education*. The Century Foundation. Retrieved from https://tcf.org/content/about-tcf/tcf-analysis-70-university-opm-contracts-reveals-increasing-risks-students-public-education/

Class Central. (2019, December 2). *By the Numbers: MOOCs in 2009*. Retrieved from https://www.classcentral.com/report/mooc-stats-2019/

Dimeo, J. (2017, August 9). Harvard Teams Up with 2U for Online Certificate Program. *Inside Higher Ed.*

Education Dive. (2020, May 13). A Look at Trends in College Consolidation Since 2016. *Education Dive.*

Gana, A. (2018, September 25). Ivory Tower in the Cloud. *Forbes.*

Garrett, R. (2018, April 19). Prove It: Do OPMs Really Boost Enrollment? *Encoura Eduventures*. Retrieved from https://encoura.org/prove-opms-really-boost-enrollment/

Grawe, N. D. (2018). *Demographics and the Demand for Higher Education*. Baltimore: Johns Hopkins University Press.

Hess, A. (2019, October 28). Harvard's Endowment Is Worth $40 Billion-Here's How It's Spent. *CNBC Make It.*

Hill, P. (2019, September 27). Online Program Management. *PhilOnEdTech.*

Hill, P. (2020, June 26). Partner, MindWires LLC (R. Ubell, Interviewer).

Holon IQ. (2019, February). Retrieved June 24, 2020, from www.holoniq.com/wp-content/uploads/2019/02/HolonIQ-Extract-Anatomy-of-an-OPM.pdf

Kim, J. (2018, August 15). 5 Things Universities Want, December from OPM Providers. *Inside Higher Ed.*

Lederman, D. (2019, October 30). Professors' Slow, Steady Acceptance of Online Learning: A Survey. *Inside Higher Ed.*

Lederman, D. (2020, March 25). The State of Online Education, Before Coronavirus. *Inside Higher Ed.*

MarcoTrends. (2020, June 22). Retrieved from www.macrotrends.net/stocks/charts/TWOU/2u/market-cap

Schwartz, N. (2020, October 20). Colleges Look to OPMs as Pandemic Intensifies Shift Online. *Education Dive.*

92   Scaling-up

Ubell, R. (2016, December 13). Why Faculty Still Don't Want to Teach Online. *Inside Higher Ed.*

Vivolo, J. (2019, July 10). Director, Online Education, Katz School of Science and Health, Yeshiva University (R. Ubell, Interviewer).

Young, J. R. (2017, September 6). Forget US News Rankings: For Online Colleges, Google Is King. *EdSurge.*

7

MOOC Invasion

In 2011, when Stanford computer scientists Sebastian Thrun and Peter Norvig came up with the bright idea of streaming their robotics lectures over the internet, they knew it was an inventive departure from the usual college course (Leckart, 2012). For hundreds of years, professors had lectured to groups of no more than a few hundred students. But MOOCs—massive open online courses—made it possible to reach many thousands at once. Through the extraordinarily vast breadth of the internet, learners could log on to video lectures streamed to wherever they happened to be.

The term, MOOC, was coined earlier in 2008 by Dave Cormier at the University of Prince Edward Island and Bryan Alexander of the National Institute for Technology in Liberal Education, remarking on an online course led by George Siemens at Athabasca University and Stephen Downes at the National Research Council of Canada (Nova Southeastern University, 2020). These early efforts, known as cMOOCs, were closer to interactive, learner-centered courses offered online by many colleges.

Familiar with the technical ingredients required for a MOOC—video streaming, IT infrastructure, and the internet—MOOC developers put code together to send lectures into cyberspace. When more than a hundred and sixty thousand enrolled in Thrun and Norvig's introduction to artificial intelligence, the professors thought they held a tiger by the tail.

94 Scaling-up

Not long after, Thrun cofounded Udacity to commercialize MOOCs, predicting that in fifty years streaming lectures would so subvert face-to-face education that only ten higher-education intuitions would remain (Leckart, 2012). Our quaint campuses would become obsolete, replaced by star faculty streaming lectures on computer screens all over the world. Thrun and other MOOC evangelists imagined they had inspired a revolution, overthrowing a thousand years of classroom teaching.

But MOOC pioneers were stunned when their online courses didn't perform anything like they had expected. At first, the average completion rate for MOOCs was less than seven percent (Parr, 2013). Completion rates then went up a bit, to a medium of about 12.6 percent, although there's considerable variation from course to course (Jordan, 2015). While a number of factors contributed to improved rates, those who paid a fee to earn a certificate showed increased chances of completion by ten to twelve points (Guest, 2019).

A more recent study by MIT researchers of more than five million students enrolled in more than twelve million MOOC courses showed that students are not doing any better (Lederman, 2019). As a matter of fact, they performed far worse than in earlier studies. New research found that for MOOC courses delivered even by MIT and Harvard faculty, completion rates fell embarrassingly to 3.13 percent, down markedly from previous results. But as expected, of those who said that they had intended to complete, as well as others who paid fees, about fifty percent stuck it out to the very end—actually not that bad, when you consider that the four-year graduation rate for students attending public universities is 33.3 percent (O'Shaughnessy, 2020).

Hunting down the data, I wondered whether we may be too fixated on completion rates. Looking closer at MOOC study habits, researchers found that some learners quit watching streaming videos in the first few minutes, while many others were merely "grazing," taking advantage of the technology to quickly log in, absorb just the morsel they were hunting for, and then log off as soon as their appetite was satisfied. Some find MOOCs useful as study guides, with learners watching videos as they would a YouTube show, supplementing in-person instruction. A great benefit of MOOCs is that students can watch as many times as it takes to clinch the point of a lesson. It turns out that most who do finish are accomplished learners, many with advanced degrees (Daly, 2013).

Writing in *EdSurge*, MOOC instructional designer Amy Ahearn says we're asking the wrong question when we seek data on completion rates to confirm their efficacy. "MOOCs should be understood as digital content, like podcasts, online magazines, Netflix series or even email campaigns, rather than facilitated educational experiences akin to college seminars." Ahearn found that "many MOOC users sign up, download the readings and workbooks, watch a select number of the videos, and even take key insights back to their team or work—but never complete and upload all of the assignments" (Ahearn, 2018). They're like music lovers who don't often listen to everything on an album, but select songs that most appeal to them, skipping all the rest. Often, connoisseurs, enamored of the style of a particular artist, pick a certain performance, listening just to the passages that are most appealing, ignoring the rest of the track.

With the totally unanticipated rush by millions to MOOCs—together with the equally surprising partnership of some of the most selective colleges— MOOCs struggled to find ways to improve their embarrassing retention rates, even though it turned out that millions of new recruits didn't seem to care very much. Even though MOOC enrollment had been slowing a bit, but owing largely to demand during the coronavirus pandemic, millions of curious new learners have signed-up recently, nibbling on the vast smorgasbord of digital classes. In the latest count, MOOCs have enrolled more than a hundred million learners (Shah, 2019).

But the two biggest MOOC providers—edX, a Harvard-MIT nonprofit joint venture, and Coursera, a Wall Street-funded start-up—recognized that completion rates matter. To improve them, they introduced a number of inducements to lure students to complete. When some learners moved up from entering courses just with a free pass to signing-up more ambitiously for paid access—which rewarded them with graded assignments and earned certificates—completion rates shot-up markedly, averaging about fifty to sixty percent, a pole-vaulting leap from single digits.

Those who enroll in edX's enterprise business track—in which companies pay for employee training—achieve even greater completion rates of nearly seventy-five percent. At Coursera, completion rates for students who earn college degrees, in partnership with notable higher ed institutions, complete at nearly ninety percent, a result startlingly greater than average on-campus student retention. A University of Michigan study of MOOC student perseverance found that paid users spent ten percent more time on their courses than classmates who took them without charge (Guest, 2019).

While the technological solution Stanford faculty had devised was novel, most MOOC innovators were unfamiliar with recent key trends in education. They knew a lot about computers and networks, but they hadn't really thought through how people learn. It's unsurprising then that the first MOOCs merely replicated the standard lecture, an uninspiring teaching

96   Scaling-up

style, but one with which the computer scientists were most familiar. As education technology consultant Phil Hill observed in *The Chronicle of Higher Education*, "The big MOOCs mostly employed smooth-functioning but basic video recording of lectures, multiple-choice quizzes, and unruly discussion forums. They were big, but they did not break new ground in pedagogy" (Hill, 2016).

Indeed, most MOOC founders were unaware that a pedagogical revolution was already underway at the nation's universities: The traditional lecture was being rejected by many scholars, practitioners, and most tellingly, tech-savvy students. MOOC advocates also failed to appreciate the existing body of knowledge about learning online, built over the last couple of decades by adventurous faculty who were attracted to online teaching for its innovative potential, such as peer-to-peer learning, virtual teamwork, and interactive exercises. These modes of instruction, known collectively as "active" learning, encourage student engagement, in stark contrast to passive listening to lectures. Indeed, even as the first MOOCs were being unveiled, traditional lectures were on their way out (see Chapter 1). Even lectures by "star" faculty were no match for active-learning sections taught by novice instructors.

The impact of active learning can be decisive. In a 2014 meta-analysis, researchers looked at 225 studies in which standard lectures were compared with active learning in undergraduate science, math, and engineering (Freeman et al., 2014). The results were unambiguous: average test scores went up about six percent in active-learning sections, while students in traditional lecture classes were 1.5 times more likely to fail than their peers engaged in active-learning.

"We've yet to see any evidence that celebrated lecturers can help students more than even first-generation active learning does," Scott Freeman, the lead author of the study, told *Wired* (Bhatia, 2014).

While streaming lectures are mostly delivered weekly, MOOC learners nonetheless are free to jump online anytime to access lessons, often accompanied by animations and simulations, documents and other digital materials. Videos are punctuated with frequent automated multiple-choice quizzes, with students encouraged to engage in large-scale, peer-to-peer online forums.

MOOCs failed to incorporate active learning approaches or other innovations in teaching and learning common in online college courses. MOOC providers had wandered into a territory they thought was uninhabited. Yet it was a place that was already well occupied by accomplished practitioners who had thought deeply and productively over the last couple of decades about how students learn online. Like poor, baffled Columbus, MOOC makers believed they had discovered a new world.

It's telling that in their latest offerings, MOOC vendors have introduced a number of active-learning innovations. In addition to automated quiz assessment, some MOOCs offer peer-review assessment in which students, following a standard rubric, evaluate and grade assignments themselves. Still, at edX, for example, the overwhelming instruction vehicle remains streaming video. Of its more than three thousand courses, video accounts for nearly ninety-five percent.

In a departure from streaming ubiquitous video, Coursera recently announced that its users can access hands-on software in more than a hundred and twenty technical courses. Delivered in partnership with Duke, Michigan, Illinois, and the University of London, software for the new unit, known as Coursera Labs, was acquired from the Bulgarian company, Rhyme Softworks, in 2019. Rhyme's virtual machines run self-paced or live sessions on common tools, such as Jupiter Notebook, RStudio, and VS Code, downloaded from any browser. Learners can build and share code, learn data-handling techniques, and absorb other skills. It's a sign that MOOCs may be shattering their video-streaming approach, acknowledging that it's time for students to move away from listening passively to lectures, as if on Netflix, and gain nuts-and-bolts competencies right on the screen.

In addition to its new, active-learning software, Coursera has also introduced more than five hundred hands-on, instructor-led activities, called Guided Projects. Launched in 2020, with another five hundred in development, these short-form lessons—typically running for less than two hours— cover such topics as creating Python programs, building HTML websites, and similar technical coaching sessions. These new approaches represent the first crack in the impenetrable MOOC video wall.

To be sure, MOOCs have been wildly successful in giving millions of people all over the world access to a wide range of subjects presented by eminent scholars at the world's elite schools. Some courses attract so many students that a seven percent completion rate still translates into several thousand students completing—greater than total enrollment at many colleges.

MOOC MONEY

After years of panning for gold in video streams, MOOCs finally hit pay dirt. From the very first, when tens of thousands came out of nowhere— like monarch butterflies migrating in the fall—to enroll in free online university classes, the big question marks hanging over massive open online

98 Scaling-up

courses was how can they survive without making money and will free MOOCs last?

At first, MOOCs were available largely free to an unlimited number of participants, but as economic realities forced vendors to reassess their unprecedented generosity, MOOCs evolved. Today, in addition to continuing to offer some course materials without charge, learners are given a menu of paid options, from modest fees for individual access, to many thousands of dollars for a degree-granting collection of MOOCs in partnership with first-ranked schools—MIT, Georgia Tech, and the University of Illinois, among others.

Since MOOCs were first released, more than nine hundred colleges and universities have jumped in, collectively offering more than eleven thousand courses. Of the top providers, Coursera is the champion with 37 million learners, followed by edX with thirty-five million. Initiated in 2013, XuetangX, the Chinese platform in third place, claims five million (Shah, 2019).

Launched with piles of cash, top MOOC providers Coursera and edX just ploughed ahead, inexplicably delivering free classes to millions without knowing where the money was going to come from. Company techies, who had figured out how to stream classes worldwide, were way ahead of C-suite executives who were still scratching their heads about how to extract cash from millions of online learners. One cynical blogger joked that giving away your product is not a very effective business model. It "does not, in general, result in much income."

Writing in *Fortune* during the dot-com boom, financial tech observer Erick Schonfeld recognized that what internet-based company CEOs "crave above all else is eyeballs . . . eyeballs mean customers." But focusing on eyeballs alone, he cautioned, makes it hard to grasp the real business question: "Is there a chance they will ever turn a profit?" (Schonfeld, 2000). To everyone's jaw-dropping surprise, MOOCs had attracted more than one hundred million learners, representing a colossal number of eyeballs.

After filling its war chest with $145 million, following three rounds of venture funding, Coursera kept hunting for the right strategy to make its vigilant investors happy—that is, turn a profit and pay handsome dividends. In July 2020, the company raised an additional $130 million, increasing its valuation to $2.5 billion. For edX, the nonprofit MIT-Harvard joint venture financed with a combined $60 million investment, nonprofit sustainability is the name of the game.

In 2021, Coursera became one of the rare edtech companies to go public, raising nearly $520 million in its initial offering. Valued at more than

$3.6 billion—a "unicorn" in Silicon Valley parlance—it has three-quarters of a billion socked away in cash (Young, 2021).

"In the beginning, we hadn't really thought out how our courses would be monetized," recalled Daphne Koller, who served as co-CEO of Coursera when it was first launched. "We just put it online for millions of learners, witnessing incredible pent-up demand." Koller is now CEO of a new video-conferencing competitor to Zoom, Engageli, built especially for the higher ed market.

After years of looking for the right formula, both Courera and edX uncovered how to turn all those eyeballs into cash, a weird twenty-first century alchemy. Meanwhile, Udacity took another path to generate revenue, offering about forty "Nanodegrees," a neologism, representing a group of career-focused, non-credit courses in such hot new fields as self-driving cars. It also delivers about two hundred free technical courses.

Long before they hit on the right money-making scheme, Coursera, edX, and other MOOC providers had set the stage for big things to come by successfully recruiting many of the world's top universities to join them. Their stunning success laid the foundation for everything that followed. It was a staggering achievement to have been able to entice, not only some of the most selective, but also among the most conservative, risk-averse institutions to share their formidable brands with these upstarts. It was an especially *Odd Couple* arrangement—MOOCs, after all, are online courses, commonly dismissed by most elite universities as inferior products.

"Coursera exceeded in attracting more university partners than I had anticipated," continued Koller, "demonstrating the value of aggregators, one-stop-shops, aimed at the broad consumer seeking alternative credentials."

Once Stanford faculty launched Coursera and Harvard and MIT partnered to introduce edX, reluctance to embrace digital education among select schools slowly gave way to grudging tolerance. The distain with which online instruction was held by senior faculty at elite colleges gradually dissolved, allowing top universities to hold their noses—so much so that eventually, Yale, École Normale Supérieure, and Peking University, together with nearly a thousand more of the world's most selective universities signed on as MOOC partners.

"Online education for degree-granting universities has been around for more than two decades, in various forms, and MOOCs are but one version," observed Phil Hill (Hill, 2016). "Nevertheless, when the founding institutions—Stanford, MIT, and Harvard—justified their investment in MOOCs, they publicly called attention to the transformative potential

100 Scaling-up

of broader online education, including its ability to improve face-to-face courses using technology."

MOOCs give elite schools cover for their resistance to go online on their own. Many jumped into the MOOC pool as long as they dove in together with A-list peers, but few offer online degrees without partnering with Coursera, edX, and other providers. Uncommonly in the Ivy League, Columbia offers a number of online engineering and doctoral degrees and the University of Pennsylvania delivers a virtual bachelor's degree for career-minded students, but neither Harvard nor any other Ivy offers a single online degree with the school's seal on the diploma (Littlefield, 2019). At highly selective schools, face-to-face is at the honored center, online at the gauche periphery.

With the surprising embrace of so many notable schools and with an immense number of enrolled learners, it was time for MOOCs to pivot. After years of treading water, not knowing where to turn, it was time for MOOCs to stop giving it all away and start making some money.

Three key ingredients accounted for transforming MOOCs into potential money-making machines. Here is their sweet-spot recipe:

Step 1: Convert your random catalog of disaggregated courses, across nearly all of scholarship, into distinct bundles of connected classes in targeted fields, say, cybersecurity or machine learning. It's particularly sweet if they happen to be in widely appealing science, technology, or business fields.

Step 2: Make sure your bundles carry college credit, and brand them with gravitas, with such seductive titles as "MicroMasters." Best of all, offer full or partial degree programs. MOOC credit bundles can often be stacked like Legos, giving students the flexibility to either go just far enough to earn a partial degree, or, if they can, go on to earn a full degree. As edX CEO Anant Agarwal acknowledged, "Credit is the gold coin of education today."

Step 3: Hang a steep, discounted tuition price tag on your credit-bearing bundles. All the while, add millions of new learners each year by continuing to deliver free courses, admittedly, without new bells and whistles offered to your paying customers. MOOC providers say they mostly split revenue with their academic partners, fifty-fifty, but also negotiate separate deals with certain schools, often sixty-forty (see Chapter 6).

Once they mixed the ingredients, it didn't take long for an expanding menu of delicious new, for-credit bundles at discounted tuition to come tumbling out of MOOC kitchens.

MOOC providers repackaged their enormous catalog of courses, converting them into series of non-degree or alternative credentials, including Specializations, MicroMasters, Nanodegrees, Professional Certificates, and XSeries. With hundreds of Specializations, co-developed with universities everywhere, Coursera also partners with corporations and research organizations.

In addition to MicroMasters, edX also offers twelve master's degree programs in partnership with Georgia Tech, Boston University, Arizona State University, and several others in the U.S. and England. Concentrated mostly in high-tech fields, such as analytics, cybersecurity, and data science, edX degrees are steeply discounted, running from about $10,000 to nearly $25,000 for degrees that commonly go for $40,000 to $60,000 on campus.

At Coursera, its MOOC ovens were also working overtime. In addition to its existing partnership with the University of Illinois—a joint venture in an iMBA and its master's degree in computer science in data science—it launched a new iMSA, a master's degree in accounting, also at Illinois, plus a new master's in innovation and entrepreneurship with the École des Hautes Études Commerciales (HES) in Paris. Today, Coursera offers more than twenty-five credit-bearing degrees in alliance with top-ranked schools at discounts similar to those offered by edX.

Former Coursera CEO Rick Levin, who moved to the company after serving as president of Yale, said that students can now "get a great education at a fraction of the cost" of earning degrees on campus.

In the United States, the biggest obstacle standing in the way of students going to college is not their high-school grades nor their test scores. It's cash. For low-income applicants especially, soaring tuition is one of the main reasons that as many as forty percent of those accepted in the spring don't show up in the fall (Kolodner, 2015).

According to the College Board, for the 2020 school year, U.S. average tuition and fees are about $37,700 at private colleges, $10,500 for state residents at public colleges, and $27,000 for out-of-state residents (College Board, 2020). To these charges, add about $10,000 per year for room and board. In general, tuition has been rising far faster than the cost of living. Going to college can be like buying a new Mercedes every year.

How did this affliction invade our universities? While there are many causes, two factors stand out. For public schools, the answer is simple: state legislatures have savaged higher education over the last decade. Previously, up to two-thirds of a state college's budget came from the state; now only about half of it does. Students and their families pick up much

102   Scaling-up

of the difference (Oliff et al., 2013). The bloating of academic bureaucracy is another cause. While the number of faculty hasn't grown much, non-academic staff at colleges and universities has ballooned—more than doubling in a generation (Richmond, 2014). What's more, compensation for administrators is often far greater than faculty pay. The painful result of the tuition epidemic is that U.S. student debt is now at an all-time peak of more than a trillion dollars.

When the first low-cost, degree-granting MOOCs appeared on the scene, they seemed like the answer to a prayer. Nelson Baker, Georgia Tech's dean of professional education, told me that scale allows the school to offer its digital degree for far less than what it charges residential students. There are about four thousand students enrolled in the school's MOOC-based computer science master's degree program, compared to the on-campus cohort of three hundred. Georgia residents pay about $20,000 per year for the on-campus program, with out-of-state tuition nearly double that. Tuition for MOOC students is just $6,630. Launched in 2014, Georgia Tech's MOOC-style master's program was the nation's first, followed recently by a Georgia Tech MOOC master's degree in data analytics.

In 2015, MIT collaborated with edX to offer what it calls a "MicroMasters." The new credential gives students who pass five graduate-level MOOC courses, plus a proctored final exam, the chance to apply for an accelerated, on-campus master's degree program that is about one-third less expensive than its on-campus equivalent. MIT's first MicroMasters was in supply chain management. While a student completing the master's degree entirely on campus pays $67,000, others who enrolled in the MicroMasters and then go on to its residential program, pay just $45,000. MIT has since rolled out several others. About thirty other colleges and universities in the U.S. and abroad have joined the parade.

This is a sea-change in the structure of higher education over the past half century. When I enrolled at Brooklyn College in the late 1950s, I paid no tuition. I remember paying merely a $200 fee for access to the gym and paying for books, of course, but apart from trolly fare from my parent's home, everything was free. In post-WWII America, college was considered a citizen's right—not a commodity to be purchased, online or otherwise, as in a supermarket.

Even as schools continue to search for ways to reduce tuition, through MOOCs or other means, the answer may come from outside of academia. Recently, Rhode Island Governor Gina Raimondo announced giving residents two years of free tuition at the state's public colleges (Miller, 2017). New York's Governor Andrew Cuomo has waived tuition for any state resident accepted at a state or city university, provided their family income is $125,000 or less (New York State, 2018). Following these and other state initiatives, President Biden has signaled his support for a national, tuition-free college program, very like the one proposed earlier by Sen. Bernie Sanders, offering free undergraduate degrees to families with incomes less than $125,000. If there's a cure for the tuition epidemic, such progressive moves seem far more promising than simply leaving it in the hands of colleges and universities.

Neither Coursera nor edX is in the black yet, but by stirring the three key ingredients—bundling, credit, and discounted tuition—there's a good chance that their trajectory is now set, moving from pin money to real money.

Steward Brand, who founded the *Whole Earth Catalog* in the 1960s, is said to have originated the slogan "Information wants to be free," an idea that eventually sparked the open-source movement, a near cousin of the first "O" in MOOCs that stands for "open"—or free (Lai, 2009). For the millions who benefited from the generosity of free MOOCs, which happily still continues, it's poignant to see some of the optimism of those early heady days succumb to the hegemony of the marketplace.

"On the one hand information wants to be expensive, because it's so valuable," Brand declared. "The right information in the right place just changes your life. On the other hand, information wants to be free, because the cost of getting it out is getting lower and lower all the time. So, you have these two fighting against each other."

ON-THE-JOB MOOCS

Over the past two decades, the great internet wave that swept through industry and revolutionized everything in its wake—including manufacturing, product development, supply chain management, marketing, financial transactions, and customer service—likewise transformed on-the-job training (Bersin, 2014). Companies eager to cut costs saw the overwhelming economic advantage of online instruction over the conventional classroom, and so they shuttered lavish country-club-style training parks and canceled employee travel to professional development courses in exotic locales. These days, most workers tend to receive their training at their desks, the better to maintain productivity.

Web instruction has also helped companies expand internationally because they can easily circulate self-learning modules to a geographically dispersed labor force at a relatively low cost. As Australian scholar

104 Scaling-up

Paul Nicholson observed, "E-learning in business and training [is] driven by notions of improved productivity and cost reduction, especially in an increasingly globalized business environment."

Over the past decade, enrollment of employees in online programs has grown twenty times faster than has student enrollment at traditional colleges and universities. By 2020, sixty percent of workers receiving tuition reimbursement were enrolled in online programs, according to EdAssist, a corporate tuition-assistance consulting firm (EdAssist, 2014).

Yet despite the corporate romance with online training for employees, companies have had a more troubled relationship with the virtual education offered by colleges and universities. When digital university programs first became available in the mid-nineties, many companies simply ignored them, refusing to provide tuition assistance to employees who enrolled in digital degree programs. Later, when it became apparent that some of the nation's most selective schools actually offered high-quality online master's degrees, especially in fields that paralleled industry needs, businesses grew more accepting.

To be sure, not every program offered a high-quality education, and a number of companies unwittingly allowed their employees to enroll in for-profit online schools that turned out to be scams (Jaffe, 2016).

"For a time, companies were not as serious about vetting universities as they are today," says Allan Weisberg, former chief learning officer at Johnson & Johnson. "When we finally looked into some for-profits, we discovered they were scams, and turned them down."

A number of Fortune 500 companies responded by setting stricter rules on their tuition-reimbursement programs to prevent unsuspecting employees from throwing away money—the company's as well as their own—on discredited programs at for-profits and other substandard schools. Other companies sensibly steered their workers toward approved universities that perform serious research paralleling the firm's own research interests and that employ significant numbers of the school's own alumni.

"Today, wise companies invest their tuition dollars in established non-profit and public schools," says Weisberg. "With stricter polices, companies want to make sure that tuition assistance is valuable to all parties—employees, corporations, and universities."

Ideally, online training should give personnel the chance to acquire new and valuable skills, perhaps in emerging fields like machine learning or data science. Such training helps the company, of course, and it also gives workers an edge in a tricky economy. Earning a degree online is also a huge convenience for workers, whose days are already filled as it is. A mid-career engineer with job, family, and travel responsibilities can more easily study online at his or her own pace—at ten at night after the kids are in bed—rather than commute to campus.

When e-learning first emerged a couple decades ago, companies turned their backs on it. But by 2014, resistance had collapsed with the conquest of swifter and cheaper virtual training over traditional methods. But just when companies started imagining that the learning industry was comfortably settled, dominated by just two principal players—classrooms and e-learning—a new competitor invaded. Out of the blue, MOOCs muscled in.

It didn't take long for talent development professionals, looking for cost-effective workforce development, to notice. By 2014, twenty-two percent had already opted for MOOCs at their organizations and thirty-six percent planned to do so, according to *MOOCs: Expanding the Scope of Organizational Learning*, a report from ATD Research and the Institute for Corporate Productivity (ATD, 2014).

Given that the switch to online job training was largely a cost-cutting move, it's only natural that when MOOCs came on the scene in 2011, companies were curious. Because they're designed to reach hundreds or thousands at once, MOOCs benefit from economies of scale that smaller online programs don't share.

Google and Instagram are experimenting with MOOC provider Coursera's Specializations, groups of related courses in key areas of interest to industry. The fee for a Coursera Specialization runs from $150 to $500 for anywhere from three to ten courses, plus a capstone project. The most popular offerings include data science, Python, and machine learning. Compared to the thousands of dollars for a more conventional training program, MOOCs are a bargain.

And if a company's aim is for workers to quickly acquire in-demand skills, rather than earning an accredited degree that may take a year or more to complete, a set of focused MOOCs may be the way to go. This skills-centered approach, known in education circles as competency-based education, is a growing trend at U.S. schools.

But before companies jump on the MOOC bandwagon, they might consider whether their ideal employee is someone with up-to-date skills in a narrow specialty, or a truly thoughtful professional who is prepared to go beyond his or her defined tasks and can adapt flexibly to new conditions and new markets. Ultimately, industry must decide who will fill the labor pipeline: an army of MOOC-trained workers or deeply talented personnel who've earned richly complex degrees from the nation's best universities.

106   Scaling-up

MOOCs will never sweep away face-to-face classrooms, nor can they take the place of more intensive and intimate online degree programs. The real contribution of MOOCs is likely to be much more modest, yet another digital education option.

For my reassessment of MOOCs, see Chapter 13.

REFERENCES

Ahearn, A. (2018, March 28). Stop Asking About Completion Rates: Better Questions to Ask About MOOCs in 2019. *EdSurge.*

ATD. (2014). *MOOCs: Expanding the Scope of Organizational Learning.* Retrieved from https://www.td.org/research-reports/moocs

Bersin, J. (2014, February 4). Spending on Corporate Training Soars: Employee Capabilities Now A Priority. *Forbes.*

Bhatia, A. (2014, May 12). Active Learning Leads to Higher Grades and Fewer Failing Students in Science, Math, and Engineering. *Wired.*

College Board. (2020). *Trends in College Pricing Highlights.* Retrieved from https://pnpi.org/college-board-trends-in-college-pricing-and-student-aid-2020/

Daly, J. (2013, December 4). 80 Percent of MOOC Students Already Have a College Degree. *EdTech.*

EdAssist. (2014). *EdAssist's Annual Review of Employer Tuition Assistance Programs.* Retrieved from https://docplayer.net/40266170-Edassist-s-annual-review-of-employer-tuition-assistance-programs-data-and-trend-analysis.html

Freeman, Scott et al. (2014, June 10). Active Learning Increases Student Performance in Science, Engineering, and Mathematics. *Proceedings of the National Academy of Sciences,* 8410–8415.

Guest, G. (2019, August 29). *Research Shows Certificates Boost MOOC Completion Rates: The University Record.* Ann Arbor: University of Michigan.

Hill, P. (2016, August 26). MOOCS Are Dead: Long Live Online Higher Education. *Chronicle of Higher Education.*

Jaffe, S. (2016, March 9). The For-Profit College Scam That These Students Are Still Paying for. *Moyers on Democracy.*

Jordan, K. (2015, June). *Massive Open Online Course Completion Rates Revisited: Assessment, Length, Attrition.* Retrieved from www.irrodl.org/index.php/irrodl/article/view/2112

Kolodner, M. (2015, August 14). Why Are Low-income Students Not Showing Up to College, Even Though They Have Been Accepted? *Hechinger Report.* Retrieved from https://hechingerreport.org/why-are-low-income-students-not-showing-up-to-college-even-though-they-have-been-accepted/

Lai, J. (2009, July 20). Information Wants to Be Free . . . and Expensive. *Fortune.*

Leckart, S. (2012, March). The Stanford Education Experiment Could Change Higher Education Forever. *Wired.*

Lederman, D. (2019, January 16). Why MOOCs Didn't Work, in 3 Data Sets. *Inside Higher Ed.*

Littlefield, J. (2019, May 6). Earn an Ivy League Degree Online. *ThoughtCo*. Retrieved from https://www.thoughtco.com/earn-an-ivy-league-degree-online-1098183

Miller, G. W. (2017, January 15). R.I. Students to Get Free Tuition for 2 Years at State Colleges, Under Raimondo Budget. *Providence Journal Newspaper*.

New York State. (2018). *Tuition-Free Degree Program: The Excelsior Scholarship*. Retrieved from https://www.ny.gov/programs/tuition-free-degree-program-excelsior-scholarship

Nova Southeastern University. (2020, July 2). *History of MOOC*. Retrieved from https://nsufl.libguides.com/c.php?g=112312&p=725994

Oliff, P. et al. (2013, March 19). *Recent Deep State Higher Education Cuts May Harm Students and the Economy for Years to Come*. Washington, DC: Center on Budget and Policy Priorities.

O'Shaughnessy, L. (2020, July 7). *Federal Government Publishes More Complete Graduation Rate Data*. Retrieved from www.insidehighered.com/digital-learning/article/2019/01/16/study-offers-data-show-moocs-didnt-achieve-their-goals

Parr, C. (2013, May 9). MOOC Completion Rates Below 7%. *Times Higher Education*.

Richmond, M. (2014, October 12). *The Hidden Half: School Employees Who Don't Teach*. Washington, DC: Thomas B. Fordham Institute.

Schonfeld, E. (2000, February 1). How Much Are Your Eyeballs Worth? *Fortune*.

Shah, D. (2019, December 2). By the Numbers: MOOCs in 2019. *Class Central*. Retrieved from https://www.classcentral.com/report/mooc-stats-2019/

Ubell, R. (2017). *Going Online*. New York: Routledge.

Young, J. (2021, March 31). Coursera Is Now a Public Company. What Does That Mean for Higher Education? *EdSurge*.

8

Going Online Abroad

Aimed at avoiding investing immense sums required to set up remote sites far from campus, a blended-learning solution I introduced about twenty years ago in partnership with two notable universities in China—Central University of Finance and Economics and the Beijing Institute of Technology—was a relatively low-cost option that offered Stevens Institute of Technology's technical degrees in China by merging online delivery with face-to-face instruction, uniquely taught by both American and Chinese faculty.

While student cultural immersion is one of the principal objectives of opening international branches, it turned out that launching our remote campus seven thousand miles away from Hoboken, NJ—where Stevens sits on the Hudson with a knock-out view of glittering Manhattan skyscrapers—totally unexpectedly our Beijing education adventure opened an entirely new world for me.

Before I was recruited to run sites in Beijing, China fell behind a dark curtain of my ignorance. Invisible to me were 1.4 billion Chinese people and a grand cultural history of dynasties and revolutions going all the way back astonishingly to 2070 BC. By contrast, the Greeks go back merely to 700 BC. Compared with China's ancient civilization, the West is just a toddler. The Shāng Dynasty alone lasted 554 years.

108

Before flying off halfway around the world to negotiate agreements with peer institutions in Beijing, I knew almost nothing about China. As a child at a leftist summer camp, we learned to sing, "Arise, ye who refuse to be bond slaves," the opening line of the Chinese Communist national anthem. I could recall crumbs of recent Chinese history—Mao, the Cultural Revolution, the Gang of Four—but otherwise, like Mao's *Little Red Book*, I knew just a series of catch phrases.

Soon after we concluded agreements with our Beijing partners, I enrolled in a class in Mandarin at The New School. I became an obsessive Amazon consumer, clicking links to books on Chinese ancient and current history. In China, I'd frequent government shops, hunting for unusual objects. As I write this, a pair of antique Chinese tomb figures—that I guess are musicians serenading their honored interred master—are standing on my desk, watching my fingers tell this story on my keyboard.

Just like most things in life, you can never guess the consequences of your decisions. I never suspected, when I first agreed to go to Beijing, that I'd pull aside a dark curtain in my own life, opening an unexpected fascination with a world I hardly knew. Of all of Confucius' wise sayings, "Real knowledge is to know the extent of one's ignorance," is perhaps the most profound.

MY CHINA EXPERIENCE

My own experience in China is instructive. Unexpectedly, just over a decade ago at Stevens Institute of Technology, a noted Chinese-American professor approached me to help him launch several online master's degrees in technical fields in Beijing.

"But I know nothing about China," I confessed. "Not sure I can be very useful."

Dismissing my ignorance, the faculty member insisted that my knowledge of online learning would be the key to unlocking what he had in mind. Aware of the enormous investment it would take to lift Stevens' academic infrastructure nearly seven thousand miles away in Beijing, he proposed an innovative, high-quality, cost-saving alternative.

A third of the courses in the program, he imagined, would be taught online by Stevens faculty; another third would be delivered in English in Beijing by Chinese faculty who had been educated in the U.S. and elsewhere outside of China. A final third would be given by Stevens faculty in brief, intensive courses in China. Like a satisfying cocktail, it was a finely blended solution. I was in.

But I initially worried how my boss would react. Would she go for it, especially since she had just that week been appointed vice president of my unit? I fretted for days over how to approach her—until I met over drinks with an old friend one evening.

"What should I say to her?" I asked him.

As if his entire career had been in preparation for my question, he responded with a brilliant suggestion, "Ask her to head your delegation to China."

In the vice president's office the next day, I expressed my misgivings about our proposed China adventure. "I'm not senior enough to negotiate with the Chinese," I ventured. "But if you join me as head of our delegation . . ."

First silence; then a glow of satisfaction radiated from her smile. "I always wanted to go to China," she beamed.

Our Chinese students did very well. Nearly all succeeded in capturing high-profile jobs at domestic and foreign high-tech companies. One young student, shy and hesitant in English when she was first admitted, delivered the valedictory address at graduation two years later in sophisticated, nearly flawless English. With her Stevens degree in hand, she landed a brilliant job—in Paris.

Of course, it didn't all go so swimmingly. We had to contend with Party functionaries who intimidated our Chinese faculty with tedious, bureaucratic trivia. Luckily, our clever Chinese students knew how to do an end-run around government internet censorship by accessing sites commonly out of reach of the Chinese.

SATELLITE CAMPUSES ABROAD

Like airline pilots, college leaders aren't known for risky behavior. On the contrary, they're a pretty cautious bunch. But when it comes to launching satellite campuses abroad, some have been flying blind.

Negotiating deals with foreign institutions, mostly in the Middle East and Asia, where 51 U.S. universities have planted college banners at 306 foreign campuses (C-BERT, 2020), you'd often think they lost their judgement.

In their rush to embrace globalization—newly in vogue in higher ed— they often turn a blind eye or retreat in shrouded silence when facing serious impediments, ignoring such inconvenient troubles as suppression of academic or religious freedom or accepting Communist Party officials in academic policy roles. Blown away by the hot Eastern winds of academic fashion, many lose their heads.

Going Online Abroad   111

In a recent report, the U.S. Government Accountability Office noted, for example, that while American universities operating in China say they generally experience academic freedom, they nonetheless contend with internet censorship. Some colleges end up practicing self-censorship so as not to offend their hosts (U.S. GAO, 2016).

Senior university officials can lose a sense of their cherished defense of liberal democracy, forgetting their commitments to academic freedom to keep partnerships going. They can look the other way out of reluctance to confront their generous partners, for instance, when visas are denied, or when Party officials demand a seat at the academic table.

A handful of British and Australian universities have been more successful in generating sizeable enrollments at their branch campuses than U.S. institutions. The University of Liverpool's Xi'an Jiaotong University, for example, has more than seven thousand students.

But for most U.S. colleges that have circled the globe to touch down in exotic places, meaningful financial rewards have been illusory. Of the more than three hundred and fifty international branch campuses listed on the website of the Cross-Border Education Research Team at the State University of New York at Albany, average enrollment abroad is merely five hundred, a very modest showing after a median period of ten years. It's unlikely that the tuition they generate is deep enough to make it financially worthwhile or provide a serious surplus to send back home. A good reason why 42 satellites have failed (C-BERT, 2020).

The invasion of American schools in the Middle East echoes eighteenth and nineteenth century economic imperialism. Today, with our professors lecturing in satellite campuses across Asia—from the Pacific to the ancient Biblical lands—we have entered a new age of U.S. academic colonialism.

Of course, colleges claim plenty of high-minded reasons for launching satellite campuses abroad. Chief among them is the recognition that the modern world is tightly interconnected, a global jigsaw puzzle that requires students to understand how pieces fit—or don't fit—together. Universities can no longer remain locked behind their charming iron gates, shut off from intellectual and cultural ferment elsewhere. Active learning about the world demands that students not only absorb global lessons from books and lectures, but they must go out and experience what's happening elsewhere. Study-abroad programs have long addressed the need, but remote branches are far more aligned academically with the home campus.

Colleges need to do some careful risk assessment before setting up branch campuses abroad. On the positive side, colleges stand to gain prestige, beat the competition, achieve global cultural awareness, realize new sources of

112 Scaling-up

revenue, and enter into new research collaborations. The dangers include the risks of undermining academic and religious freedom, potential loss of investment funds, waste of human capital, and confrontations with autocratic states—and most troubling to some administrators, damaging the university's prestige when things don't go well.

The University of Groningen, in Holland, must have performed a similar assessment when it canceled plans to open a branch campus in China recently, concluding that "there were a number of risks that have not been sufficiently thought through," while noting that the benefits were "difficult to quantify" (Redden, 2018).

Writing in the online journal, *The Conversation*, Gavin Moodie at RMIT University in Australia, an institution with nearly 7,000 students at a branch campus in Vietnam, said that "international branch campuses are one of the biggest reputational and financial risks universities take" (Moodie, 2015).

Not listed among the pluses and minuses are all sorts of unspoken motivations—especially the personal drama of senior faculty and staff flying off to remote spots around the globe to fall in with exotic counterparts wearing long white Emirati robes, returning triumphant with a lavish contract.

Now let's imagine a senior U.S. university official, sitting at a conference table in a sparkling glass office tower, with a gloriously undulating desert stretching far off. Across the table sits a Near Eastern government official. They are close to signing an agreement to set a U.S. satellite campus on a piece of land nearby.

But the test comes when facing the document in front of them, the government official on the other side hesitates before initialing one last paragraph, permitting faculty and students from all religions and all nations to travel freely in and out of the country to study or perform research at the new campus.

In that fraught situation, I urge the campus leader to say that unless they come to an agreement on this point, the administrator should slip the unsigned document embossed with the U.S. university's prestigious name into a briefcase, latch it, and fly home.

INTERNATIONAL ONLINE STUDENTS

International students represent about five percent of the more than twenty million enrolled in the nation's colleges and universities. In the last decade, according to Moody's Investors Service, the number of students from overseas increased markedly, by more than seventy percent (Moody's, 2019). At many colleges, heavily dependent on tuition revenue, international students represent the difference between solvency and ruin. While American universities have courted international students for intellectual and cultural diversity, their contribution to the bottom line has not gone unnoticed by higher education financial officers (see Chapter 5).

But in 2020, in the midst of the coronavirus, the Institute of International Education found that international enrollment fell sixteen percent between fall of 2019 and fall of 2020. Prospects for new international students were even grimmer, with a forty-three percent fall off (Cardoza, 2020).

Typically, foreign undergraduates receive little to no financial aid and pay top-dollar in tuition. Before the pandemic, when international travel stalled, college students from overseas contributed about $39 billion to the nation's economy, helping sustain many colleges and universities (NAFSA, 2018). Foreign students have helped public colleges fill gaps left by deep cuts in state support.

Over generations, the world has looked to U.S. higher education as the best anywhere, to a large extent because it embraced diversity and welcomed students and scholars from across the globe. If I were a parent, say, in Indonesia, eager for my daughter to apply to Stanford University, I might hesitate today, thinking that she might be better off at the University of Adelaide, even though my heart is set on sending her to a top-ranking American university.

If you go to Adelaide's home page, under a banner headline, "Welcome new students," you'll see a bright smile on a young, attractive woman wearing a hijab. Universities in Canada report a surge of applications. Some quickly extended deadlines to foreign students. Rebecca Grappo, president of RNG International, an education consulting firm, says that many overseas families, once eager to have their children admitted to an American college, are now taking a serious look at applying elsewhere.

Of course, Stanford and other notable universities with deep pockets will surely survive the enrollment decline of international students following the 2020 pandemic, but what about mid-market colleges with threadbare endowments whose existence crucially depends on tuition from foreign students? Most colleges and universities do not have an alternative to withstand the shock. But institutions that have introduced online programs may be better prepared to sustain the blow.

INTERNATIONAL STUDENTS ONLINE

To balance academic budgets, increasing tuition is one obvious, but perilous, source of funds, turning state institutions from easily affordable to

114 Scaling-up

a stretch for many families. With top tuition dollars coming from out-of-state and international enrollments, public higher education has recently been accused of turning away from its historic mission of laying down the stepping-stones for poor and working-class kids to enter the middle class.

Since the invasion of COVID-19, with severe travel restrictions imposed by the U.S. and other countries, international student tuition revenue has been limited and may even disappear while virus containment rules continue to be in effect—and possibly long afterward, too. Even if global travel returns, the great college migration to American colleges of students from abroad—China and India, especially—is likely to be stalled or may even be depleted by souring relations between the U.S. and China and other nations.

With about one million foreign students enrolled in U.S colleges, their tuition represents a major line item, totaling about $9 billion a year, or nearly a third of the country's college tuition revenue—decisive in maintaining the economic viability of U.S. higher education—before foreign students flew home in the pandemic. As expected, international student enrollment declined, with eleven percent disappearing in the 2020 fall semester and who knows when they will come back?

While the international student population represents a big part of the college residential population—and a major decline in foreign student enrollment is a severe blow to higher ed—few foreign students enroll in U.S. online classes. At programs of which I am familiar, foreign students represent a relatively small share of the online student population, perhaps five percent—or ten percent, at most. (I failed to uncover any reliable data on international online student enrollment in the U.S.)

Of course, the flow of foreign students in the U.S. represents a thirst to study at American colleges and universities; but international students come here—when there are no travel restrictions—not only to gain academic knowledge or to earn an American degree, but also—and very likely what attracts them most—due to the desire to be immersed in U.S. culture and, for some, the chance to secure a career-boosting position at a local company upon graduation. Rarely are any of these wishes, beyond gaining academic knowledge, fulfilled online.

Still, investing in new digital programs as a hedge against the loss of international applicants is not foolproof. Many foreign students come to the U.S., not only to earn an American degree, but equally to embed themselves in American culture, to absorb its lessons, hoping to gain marketability abroad after graduation. Others aim eventually to enter our domestic workforce to achieve scholarly or commercial success here, often unobtainable at home.

For many students from abroad, who thrive on personal networks, built on one's family relationships, school friends, neighbors, and co-workers, online study doesn't feel right. For Chinese students especially, *guanxi*, an idea originating with Confucianism emphasizing mutual obligations, reciprocity, and trust, seems antithetical to virtual education.

Will American universities be able to convince international students to enroll in what they perceive as doubtful online degrees? Will they be able to attract those turned away from coming here?

It turns out that some of the most alluring qualities that motivate domestic applicants to enroll in virtual programs are the very same that appeal to international students, with convenience rising to the very top. Just like U.S. students, who must confront life's stubborn twenty-first century obstacles—family obligations, frequent travel, and demanding jobs—many abroad are equally unable, even in their home countries, to attend class on campus, let alone fly off far from home to a school in the U.S. For foreign applicants—no different from our local students—faced with similar struggles, earning a virtual degree is ideal, since it gives them the flexibility to participate at their own pace, taking virtual classes at two in the morning. At a graduation party, a senior Indian banking executive, who had just earned her master's degree in cybersecurity online from New York University's School of Engineering, tearfully confided in me about how grateful she was that she could take her courses virtually from home where she was caring for her elderly mother.

Typically, in Asia and elsewhere abroad, students sit dutifully in class, furiously typing into laptops as professors lecture, with rare, if any, breaks for classroom discussion. Faculty authority is the accepted norm. What often draws foreign students to our colleges and universities is the appeal of American-style education. In online classes, perhaps even more than in our classrooms, faculty tend to encourage student participation and engagement, qualities that can go a long way to tempt foreign applicants, intrigued by more liberal American methods, to overcome their resistance to digital education.

For American universities to attract foreign students to their online programs, perhaps one of the most obstinate myths to puncture is the widely held notion that virtual learning is an alienating, machine-like environment, in which students act autonomously in isolated virtual classrooms like robots in a science fiction film. The fact is, however, that in a typical classroom on campus, you can sit all semester next to a classmate, nearly elbow-to-elbow, and walk out after your final exam, never having said a word to her, not knowing her name.

116 Scaling-up

Online, that estranged experience is next to impossible, since virtual instruction often demands routine participation in which you and your classmates are required to interact often, posting comments on digital message boards, in forums, by e-mail, and other peer-to-peer communications, held as if your virtual classmates were writing letters to each other, mirroring Victorian correspondence or texting friends on your smart phone.

Massive open online courses, with more than ten million enrolled in China alone, have unexpectedly emerged as the single most myth-shattering advertisement for virtual learning. Now that millions of learners abroad have tasted forbidden fruit, this may be just the right moment to attract foreign MOOC-adopters to your online degree program.

With nearly a third of U.S. students now taking at least one virtual course (or about six million students), colleges and universities without an online strategy may be cutting themselves off from the next wave of local and international digital students, replacing the disappearance of residential international enrollments. As the U.S. retreats from foreign students, many abroad may be able to earn a degree from your college online, helping to steady your rocky academic ship. Online, foreign students enter American colleges without obtaining a visa, leaping over airport Border Patrol officers, to take their seats in your institution's virtual classroom anywhere in the world.

REFERENCES

Cardoza, K. (2020, December 2). Enrollment by International Students in U.S. Colleges Plummets. *GBH News.*

C-BERT. (2020). *Cross-Border Research Team.* International Campuses Survey. Retrieved from https://cbert.org/

Moodie, G. (2015, October 11). Branching Out: Why Universities Open International Campuses Despite Little Reward. *The Conversation.*

Moody's Investment Service. (2019, November 11). *Annual Higher Education Net Revenue Growth Dropping for Public and Private Universities.* Moody's Investment Service. Retrieved from https://www.moodys.com/research/Moodys-Annual-higher-education-survey-shows-net-tuition-revenue-growth-PBM_1202552

NAFSA. (2018. November 13). International Students Contribute $39 Billion to U.S. Economy. NAFSA. *PRNewswire.*

Redden, E. (2018, February 23). Canceling Plans for a China Campus. *Inside Higher Ed.*

U.S. Government Accounting Office. (2016, August 29). *Universities in China Emphasize Academic Freedom but Face Internet Censorship and Other Challenges.* Retrieved from https://www.gao.gov/products/gao-16-757

9

Finding and Keeping Online Learners

Colleges and universities are struggling to keep students focused long enough to graduate within a reasonable amount of time after they first enroll. In the U.S., only about sixty percent of undergraduates earn their degrees in six years (National Center for Educational Statistics, 2020). The rest commonly face a blizzard of troubles—added debt, poor job prospects, and, in some cases, lack of self-worth.

While one of the biggest causes of dropping out is money—especially as the cost of college rises—that is not the only hurdle (Shankie, 2014). It turns out that in ways that are not always well understood by the public, colleges themselves share a good deal of the blame. Too often, schools have adopted a division-of-labor approach with their recruitment and retention efforts.

There is an art and science, of course, to finding students on the internet. Recruitment officials are trained to exploit the remarkable firepower of social media, vast databases, and other highly effective digital tools. They can reach millions of prospective students just by clicking the right link and paying search engines enough cash. But what happens when large numbers of new recruits enroll, only to trip and fall off their academic track.

A dozen years ago, when I first came to New York University, I found that a marketing vendor, hired by my predecessor, had been enrolling a surprising number of new online master's students. Impressed, I turned to my staff, wondering how many who had signed-up had persisted.

118   Scaling-up

"Let's look at the spreadsheets," I proposed. Taken aback by results show-ing that of the dozens of new recruits the company had attracted, only a handful had returned for the next semester. The drop-off was shocking.

College recruiters focus on generating big sign-ups to achieve their tar-gets. Concentrating solely on generating big numbers, recruiters tend to have little or no investment in what happens next. Throwing everything you have at recruitment while neglecting ways of keeping students on the path to graduation is irresponsible, especially considering the debt students often take on to enter college.

HOLISTIC ALTERNATIVE

Recruiting students to enroll online is merely the beginning of an institu-tion's more serious responsibility. The much broader objective is to make it possible for students, despite obstacles along the way, to engage in their studies over the long haul successfully, leading ultimately to graduation. At its best, recruitment and marketing continue over students' life cycles, mak-ing sure they don't fall off, but persevere with help and guidance.

To achieve greater student retention and graduation rates than is com-mon, a university's skills must go beyond basic recruitment and marketing competencies, including, especially, expertise in monitoring at-risk stu-dents, providing online student services and other strategies that engage digital learners intellectually as well as emotionally to keep them on track. It's a college's ethical obligation to do whatever is best for students to achieve their academic aims.

What if new recruits' next steps were guided by the same staff who encouraged them to sign-up in the first place? What if recruiters stayed close to apprehensive newcomers, sticking with them through orientation, helping them untangle course selection, and shepherding them through the dozens of challenges that lay ahead? What if those who struggled with stu-dents from the start of their academic journey accompanied them all the way through to commencement?

Colleges should concentrate less on enrollment efforts and more on a student's life cycle. Introducing a holistic strategy, recruiters are given a longer-term mission than just rounding-up freshmen. Colleges need to add a crucial set of competencies to recruiters' job descriptions—the skills of a retention specialist.

"Students get very close to those who recruit them," said Lisa Bellantu-ono, director of graduate admissions at the George Washington University School of Business. "Then, suddenly, at most colleges, they're cut-off from someone who knows them well and passed on to others who don't. They become just numbers in the system—totally disconnected."

A pro at student support, Bellantuono worked closely with me at NYU's engineering school. During her tenure there, her holistic method out-performed average retention and graduation rates at most engineering schools—on campus and online. Our students achieved a ninety-two per-cent retention rate and graduation rates of nearly eighty percent.

"Those best at propelling student retention are terrific at customer ser-vice," Bellantuono said. "No task is too small, no question out of bounds. Their priority is to help students achieve their goals."

In Bellantuono's approach, recruiters engage effectively with prospec-tive learners and then extend their involvement beyond enrollment, offer-ing continuing support after they sign up. In this expanded role, they help learners navigate often treacherous academic waters, guiding them through mystifying curriculum requirements, baffling financial-aid bureaucracy and obscure rules that can quickly throw students off.

These hurdles can trip-up eighteen-year-olds, for sure, and they can derail adult students as well. It's even worse for first-generation learners or online students without a face-to-face connection to campus.

"Faculty members are often the most direct way to help at-risk students," says Carl J. Strikwerda, former president of Elizabethtown College, located in the Lancaster area of Pennsylvania, in an opinion column (Stikwerda, 2019). "No matter what else colleges and universities do for students, suc-cess in the classroom is essential."

The answer is not to rely on faculty members alone, though a sympathetic professor or a trusted academic advisor may step in from time to time to help. But faculty members are not buddies. Surely, they have other pressing obligations, principally to make sure learners absorb their lessons. Other staff should be available to make sure students stay on track.

Retention and graduation rates will rise only when higher education applies a softer, more student-centered approach, rather than allowing stu-dents to sink or swim. This is not merely a practical solution to the nation's retention crisis, but a socially responsible way to run the university.

CONVENIENCE

Just try calling your college's general number to see what happens. Good luck!

Your first encounter may be: "No one is here right now to take your call, but if you leave your name and number someone will get back to you

120 Scaling-up

shortly"—a sign of dysfunctional inconvenience caused by school bureaucracy, with each unit's requirements coming first, before student convenience. A fairly common occurrence at many of the nation's colleges and universities.

On the opposite end of the inconvenience spectrum are companies who have honed their customer service through thousands of interactions to create enterprise-level support. Some weeks ago, I had trouble figuring out how to open an account at a nearby company, so I went online and clicked the firm's number I found on its homepage. "I'd like to open an account," I said, explaining to a recorded message what I had in mind. Soon afterward, I was on my way with the information I needed.

My call to the company did not go to a telephone receptionist working for, say, human resources or information technology, but to a voice-activated program representing all the company's departments—a customer-centric service equipped to respond to any question. That's why my query was handled quickly, accurately, and conveniently—unlike the support you may find at a college call center.

"Higher education has not yet figured it out," Peggy McCready, former associate vice provost for technology and digital initiatives at the University of Pennsylvania Libraries, recently told me. "Service and support at universities are not up to the level of personalization we've grown accustomed to at the drugstore, where your prescription is refilled automatically and you're reminded when you haven't picked it up."

One reason, she argues, is that colleges and universities are often radically decentralized, making the standard of service different in different campus departments and sectors. "With a more diverse student population, nontraditional students, without helpful and easily accessible tools, struggle to find resources they need to succeed."

"Siloed university units are dinosaurs that are fast becoming extinct," predicts Ryan Craig in *Forbes* (Craig, 2017). "By getting rid of organizational silos and focusing on how to best serve students—from applicants' first interactions through decades as alumni—students and universities win."

A couple of decades ago at Stevens Institute of Technology, we polled our digital students about why they chose to enroll as virtual learners. Did they come to our virtual classrooms for the strength of our faculty? Quality of the program? Reputation of the college?

When we tallied the results, one reason emerged as a driving force for our online learners: they came seeking convenience.

We shouldn't have been surprised. Noted Columbia University legal scholar, Tim Wu, has called convenience, "the most underestimated and least understood force in the world today" and "perhaps the most powerful force shaping our individual lives and our economies" (Wu, 2018).

Of course, technology has brought new conveniences for on-campus as well as online students. Back when I was an undergraduate at Brooklyn College, for example, each semester I'd queue up for hours in the school gym in front of long tables with blank-faced staff to register for class. I'd fret that my longed-for Shakespeare class would close-out by the time I finally reached the front of the line.

Today, students register painlessly from their dorm, home, or anywhere with their laptop or smartphone. And that is what students now expect, since digital services have practically eliminated standing in line anywhere. Raised on apps and on-demand media, students can access almost anything, merely by keying a link. But these days, colleges can be left behind in their digital services.

Inconvenience—like forcing students to rush around campus from one dean's office to another for approvals—neither builds character nor imparts learning but inflames exasperation with a college's inattention to student needs. Student life is complicated and stressful enough without adding unnecessary obstacles.

"As consumers, convenience is one of students' key expectations, but not often realized on campus," said academic IT guru Lev Gonick, Arizona State University's CIO. "Even so, convenience is a huge and basic student expectation. Wrap-around services make students feel they are very much part of the university."

Students are often baffled by the dizzying academic options confronting them in the school catalog, puzzled as to what program or course to choose. But figuring out how to navigate non-academic departments and services can be equally bewildering.

That's why a few years ago, Arizona State University launched a mobile app, an online one-stop shop, helping students maneuver on-campus services and decisively providing robust student engagement. I logged on and was dazzled by how simple and easy it was to locate nearly everything students might need.

With just one click, students can access the school's academic calendar, library, or any one of dozens of other sites. They can view campus maps showing bus routes, stops, and schedules, as well as shuttle services. They can click on entertainment options available right on the app. Troubled students

122   Scaling-up

can even call ASU's Counseling Services to speak directly to a counselor—without an appointment.

ASU students have now downloaded it 130,000 times, accessing it more than 3.4 times a day to check class schedules, navigate campus services, or see student alerts—all in the palm of their hands. Thanks to an integration with TicketMaster, it gives students access to ASU football games.

Many colleges, aware of the changing needs of the student population today, are installing collaborative maker spaces, student-run print shops, convenience stores, and in a science-fiction departure at UC Berkeley, a robot-run food delivery service to student dorms.

Raised on quick responses from smartphones, social media, instant messaging, and immediate-access entertainment sites, today's students live in an on-demand world. Click on anything and get it immediately. It's a world in which no one needs to wait in line anymore, or even go somewhere to shop. A world in which Amazon will send you any product you're looking for from the largest virtual mall ever imagined.

The doorman in my apartment building no longer sits amiably at his station, pleasantly greeting residents and visitors; he's now a shipping clerk, barricaded by giant stacks of pale brown cardboard boxes, many printed with a long black curve of a smile. With the massive number of deliveries being made, every day is Christmas in my building.

One place on campus that has been quickest to bring in conveniences has been the library, where paper card catalogs were long ago retired, replaced by digital searching. "The importance of convenience is especially prevalent among younger generations in their studies, but is true across all demographic categories—age, gender and academic role," concludes a recent report from OCLC, the giant library technology cooperative (Connaway, 2015).

And for plenty of students, college is just not possible unless it is made convenient enough to fit into the limited time and space they have to devote to studies. That's especially true for students working full-time jobs, for parents caring for children, and for others who cannot just hop into their cars and drive off to a campus. That's why online programs at colleges have also been a leader in focusing on convenience.

Of course, there's no guarantee that digital replacements for onerous tasks will be simpler or easier to use. Just recently, it took me more than twenty minutes, with several failed attempts, to submit student grades to an awkwardly designed online form that would have been a snap with just pencil and paper. And no one is spared the frustration, waiting while rudely long, irritating tunes keep you on hold, in attempting to right some trivial, but hostile, digital error. Flaws in online convenience can turn into a nightmare of dysfunction.

There are those who think that convenience is just an expensive trick, exploited by capitalism to circulate commodities faster than ever to increase profit. Like Sirens in *The Odyssey*, consumerism seduces our desires—envy, fame, or happiness, and love—compelling our keyboard fingers to click open our credit cards faster than ever.

"Making things easier isn't wicked," argues Columbia's Wu. "On the contrary, it often opens up possibilities that once seemed too onerous to contemplate, and it typically makes life less arduous, especially for those most vulnerable to life's drudgeries."

For scholars and academic leaders who encourage young minds to explore philosophy, science, and other heady pursuits, focusing on student convenience may seem a foolishly trivial detour from what matters most. Yet ignoring convenience could send college students fleeing to more accommodating places that pay more attention to what they need.

We owe our students convenience for the respect it represents, the sanity it embraces, and the kindness it demonstrates. And for some colleges that face falling enrollments, becoming more convenient may be a key to survival—just like the shops along my street that have been threatened by Amazon and other online alternatives.

REFERENCES

Connaway, L. (2015). *The Library in the Life of the User*. Dublin, OH: OCLC. Retrieved from www.oclc.org/content/dam/research/publications/2015/oclcresearch-library-in-life-of-user.pdf

Craig, R. (2017, April 24). College Silos Must Die for Students to Thrive. *Forbes*.

National Center for Educational Statistics. (2020, April). *Undergraduate Retention and Graduation Rates*. Retrieved from https://nces.ed.gov/programs/coe/indicator_ctr.asp

Shankie, E. (2014, October 23). Dropout Rate for College Students Driven by Income Inequality. *Nonprofit Quarterly*.

Stikwerda, C. (2019, September 4). Faculty Members Are the Key to Solving the Retention Challenge. *Inside Higher Ed*.

Wu, T. (2018, February 16). The Tyranny of Convenience. *New York Times*.

Section 4
Problems and Considerations

10

Online Cheating

Spooked by horror stories of an online cheating plague, how should university faculty members and administrators respond? Should they launch a virtual anti-cheating crusade, armed with high-tech surveillance, ending in disciplinary terror—retribution, chastisement, and sanctions, marked by failing grades and expulsions? Or should they just throw up their hands in defeat, treating it as a chronic academic illness, no worse in our lecture halls and online than outside the campus gates, with integrity equally under siege by marriage infidelities, corporate malfeasance, and irresponsible politicians playing fast and loose with "alternative facts"?

Even though cheating is relatively common on campus—between fifty to sixty percent of U.S. college students say that they cheated at least once (LaBeff, 1990)—one of the first suspicions raised by those skeptical of virtual education is: isn't there more cheating online than in face-to-face instruction?

Without any data to back them up, most doubters quickly conclude that virtual dishonesty is endemic, far worse online than in traditional classrooms. But the paradoxical truth is that a handful of studies unexpectedly report that there is less of it happening online than on campus; with some saying there is no significant difference between the two (Stuber-McEwen et al., 2009). I was astonished myself when I discovered these surprising results while researching this chapter.

127

128   Problems and Considerations

Looking for blame, we tend to accuse students of being more untrustworthy now than ever, or we denounce the wider society as more corrupt, the source of moral decline. But my guess is that students—online or face-to-face—are no more unethical now than they once were, nor is society more depraved today than in earlier times. History has a way of uncovering far worse behavior—say, in Victorian times or—than in our own. The fact is, despite our belief that our permissive age gives students more license to transgress than ever, over a number of years, the rate of academic dishonesty has stayed pretty much the same.

In a cascade of studies, serious scholars have tried to unearth what in student psychology, or in our collective environment, moves students to cheat. Some identify deep ethical lapses; others point to more common causes—peer and parental pressure, grade anxiety, competition, resentment of authority, feelings of unfairness, and so on. While conventional wisdom seems to agree with the scholarly literature—that there are psychological and social reasons why students cheat—nonetheless, we might do better to turn our attention in the other direction. Rather than investigate *student* behavior, it may be far more illuminating to see what *faculty members* are doing.

To my mind, cheating is more a consequence of conventional classroom instruction, an exhausted pedagogy that has long since outlived its effectiveness. Most of the nation's colleges and universities are still stuck in a century-old, faculty-centered style, forcing students to parrot their teachers in midterms and final exams, as if mass memorization is the object of education. Radical Brazilian education innovator Paolo Freire long-ago ridiculed traditional teaching for its "banking concept of education," with students dutifully memorizing content, turning them into instructional depositories (Freire, 1970).

Instead of subjecting students to a pair of menacing tests each semester—midterms and finals—research has shown that instructors can seriously reduce test-taking anxiety by administering low-stakes quizzes, distributed frequently throughout the term. With low-stakes quizzes, rather than high-stakes summative exams, students reveal the cumulative results of learning over time, rather than inflated outcomes drawn from all-nighters.

Like an intravenous feed, rather than the stab of an injection, the mind absorbs lessons drip-by-drip, not in a single shot. With frequent, relaxed tests, facts and ideas are more likely to be retained long after grades are posted, while binge studying for high-stakes exams can easily evaporate on the last day of class.

Nineteenth-century German psychologist Hermann Ebbinghaus first noticed that when learning is divided into a number of short periods over a long time, rather than in one long round, in a phenomenon known as *spacing practice,* results are commonly more effective than intense study (Ebbinghaus, 2014). *Massed practice,* consisting of fewer, longer sessions, often ends in poorer outcomes. In one study reporting on the value of low-stakes quizzes, students who took a series of quizzes during the semester performed significantly better than those who didn't. Since not much rides on a chain of low-stakes quizzes—especially when they are not counted as central to your grade—there's no reason to scribble answers on the inside of water-bottle labels or mark your forearm with your ball-point, an academic tattoo hidden under your long-sleeved shirt. Why cheat, if there's so little at stake?

To reduce test-taking anxiety even more, prudent instructors divide instruction into small chunks. With this approach, online students are graded on a long series of tasks—homework assignments, message-board participation, virtual exercises, teamwork roles, and low-stakes quizzes, among other things with no single element dominating any other, reflecting student performance, not in one or two make-or-break wrap-up exams.

With one click, virtual instructors can easily distribute frequent quizzes. They can also quickly update and change exam questions, preventing students from posting questions and answers online. Most learning management systems give faculty the ability to randomize test questions so that no two students receive exactly the same exam. Tech companies like ProctorU and Tegrity offer remote proctoring, with company staff monitoring test-takers with screen-sharing and webcam feeds. Recently, new keystroke biometric software measures the uniqueness of student keyboard typing, a white-hat hacker's sci-fi dream.

On campus, primitive surveillance—no cameras, just human vision—is the most common and relatively porous cheating-prevention tactic. The bored and uncertain gaze of faculty or graduate students is the university's principal permeable defense. In large lecture halls, rarely, if ever, does anyone ask students to show their identity cards, allowing anyone to slip into your place. Online, you can't take your virtual exam without showing your driver's license or student ID to your virtual proctor.

During the coronavirus outbreak, the sheer number of online students may have undermined the integrity of virtual proctoring. ProctorU reports that because the pandemic forced millions of students online, virtual cheating rose to an unprecedented eight percent. Before the crisis, the company found that cheating online was so rare, it represented fewer than one percent of the 340,000 exams it conducted from January through March 2020.

130 Problems and Considerations

During the height of remote testing, the company says, the number of exams it ran jumped to 1.3 million from April through June of the same year (Newton, 2020). "We can only imagine what the rate of inappropriate testing activity is when no one is watching," said Scott McFarland, chief executive of ProctorU.

No strategy—however seemingly foolproof—is safe from inventive students or commercial interlopers from gaming the system. Some of the ways students devise to do an end-run around online exams are so ingenious that their brilliance would have been better spent actually studying and taking the exam—and very likely acing it.

REFERENCES

Ebbinghaus, H. (2014). *Memory: A Contribution to Experimental Psychology*. New York: Windham.

Freire, P. (1970). *Pedagogy of the Oppressed*. New York: Bloomsbury.

LaBeff, E. (1990, April). Situational Ethics and College Student Cheating. *Sociological Inquiry*, 60.

Newton, P. (2020, August 7). Another Problem with Shifting Education Online: A Rise in Cheating. *Washington Post*.

Stuber-McEwen, D. et al. (2009, Fall). Point, Click and Cheat: Frequency and Type of Academic Dishonesty in the Virtual Classroom. *Online Journal of Distance Learning Administration*, 12(3).

11

Online Predators

This chapter merges previously published articles on Betsy DeVos' tenure at the U.S. Department of Education. Since the election of Joe Biden, a new administration is now running the department. Many of the actions described will likely be reversed. Nevertheless, it's useful to remember what happened not long ago. Even so, recent data shows that for-profits are on the rise again, with enrollment up three percent in 2020 (Cellini, 2020).

In the wild, predators often prey on the weak, attacking the young, sick, and injured. In online education, Wall Street for-profit universities also go after the most vulnerable, often leaving hapless students with insupportable debt and few marketable skills. Predators in the wild hunt and kill out of biological necessity; cruelly, for-profits go in for the kill to make a buck.

James Surowiecki, a *New Yorker* finance columnist, says for-profits "invested heavily in online learning, which enabled them to operate nationwide and to keep costs down" (Surowiecki, 2015). Of the 1.3 million enrolled in for-profit colleges, online students represent about thirteen percent.

With a college education as the enticing brass ring for those who fall off the American dream merry-go-round, for-profits, exploiting shrewd—often deceptive—come-ons, promise a second chance for many who don't think

131

132 Problems and Considerations

they can get into a local college or university. Students enrolled in for-profits tend to be at higher risk—older, poorer, minority, nontraditional. Under the gun, they suffer from a barrage of blows: serious drop-out rates (with some as high as 66 percent), higher tuition than at state schools, appalling student-loan default rates, and, worst of all, miserably poor post-graduation employment (Sharp et al., 2017).

A Brookings Institution report (Looney and Yannelis, 2015) claims that the student loan crisis in the U.S. "is largely concentrated among nontraditional borrowers attending for-profit schools and other non-selective institutions, who have relatively weak educational outcomes and difficulty finding jobs after starting to repay their loans. In contrast, most borrowers at four-year public and private nonprofit institutions have relatively low rates of default, solid earnings, and steady employment rates." For-profit student debt has grown from $39 billion in 2000 to $229 billion in 2014. While they account for just fifteen percent of U.S. college students, for-profit students—on campus or online—are responsible for nearly half of all loan defaults.

Much of the debt is fueled by federal support for students who can't afford increasingly stiff tuition at the nation's universities. Pell grants and other programs step in to allow low-income families to send their kids to college. Insidiously, corporations wormed their way into this federal slush fund. A U.S. Senate committee report revealed that fifteen Wall Street funded for-profit education companies received nearly ninety percent of federal tuition-assistance programs (Looney, 2015). In 2009–2010, for-profit colleges received $32 billion from these programs, 25 percent of the total spent at all colleges and universities in the U.S. The other major source of federal money for for-profit schools comes from military and veteran tuition assistance benefits.

For-profits have failed to propel the economic and status levels of their students, a socially productive force that U.S. colleges have historically promised the middle and working classes. Instead, for-profit students remain stuck—and probably worse off—than they were before they signed up because now, they're saddled with unsustainable student loans. As the son of an immigrant tailor, had I gone to a for-profit, rather than Brooklyn College, then a free city university, chances are I would not have held jobs at New York University and other academic and commercial institutions in my career.

For-profits have no financial interest in nurturing students, in helping them graduate or get good jobs. Just like magazine promotion schemes in the old print days that thrived on accumulating subscribers, rather than readers, corporate higher education makes its money on the "churn," unconcerned with how many get through to the end, focusing their enormous Wall

Street resources and superior digital marketing skills at the front end—on the thousands who enroll and pay tuition up front. If your principal interest is in generating big enrollments fast, why would you care if students actually learned anything or went on to live a purposeful life?

As commercial entities, for-profits don't enroll students, but customers, with courses offered as products. A U.S. Senate report documents how disgracefully the churn works. More than sixty percent of students who enrolled in the University Phoenix in 2008–2009 dropped out in four months in the middle of 2010, leaving them not only without a diploma, but disheartened (Simon and Emma, 2014). Alert to the dangers, the previous administration stepped in to protect the helpless. In a muscular campaign to reduce the force of for-profits, former U.S. Department of Education Secretary Arne Duncan declared, "We want to protect students from enrolling in poorly performing programs that leave them with debt they cannot pay and a degree they cannot use."

In a cynical about-face from its campaign, buddying-up to working-class voters, the Trump administration sought to open the gates, permitting the return of predators—with open season to exploit the defenseless citizens who elected them. Almost immediately, U.S. Secretary of Education Betsy DeVos moved to dismantle key elements of the government's protective apparatus.

DELAY AND RENEGOTIATE KEY PROVISIONS OF THE GAINFUL-EMPLOYMENT RULE

The Obama-era gainful employment regulation penalizes programs whose student loan payments exceed a set percentage of graduates' earnings. If learners—residential or digital—borrow money to attend a for-profit but end up unable to find jobs that allow them to re-pay the loans comfortably, the program is marked as "failing" and could lose access to federal financial aid. About three hundred for-profits buckled under the rule and shut down (Mayotte, 2015).

DELAY AND RENEGOTIATE THE BORROWER-DEFENSE RULE

A regulation that was supposed to take effect in 2017, but was put on hold, gives defrauded borrowers the right to apply for loan forgiveness. It also assures students in closed schools that they will have their loans forgiven. The giant for-profit company, Corinthian, is a prime example. It shut down,

134 Problems and Considerations

leaving more than ten thousand students stranded. Merely three thousand of them so far have had their loans forgiven. Altogether, Corinthian students owe more than $3 billion.

HIRE FORMER AGGRESSIVE FOR-PROFIT EXECUTIVES

One example is the hiring of Robert S. Eitel, a top executive at Bridgepoint Education, a big for-profit college company. Senior counselor to Secretary DeVos, Eitel was the department's regulatory reform officer whose job it was to trim rules that protect students. Writing in the "Upshot" column of *The New York Times*, commentator Kevin Carey concluded that when the Obama-era rules are decimated, "Ms. DeVos will have destroyed a highly effective tool for protecting students from for-profit colleges that offer few job prospects and mountains of debt" (Carey, 2017).

Corporations have invaded nearly every sector of the nation's economic life, unnaturally in zones where we once imagined capitalism had no place—day care, hospitals, nursing homes, prisons, and our universities. So, let's nail a "do not enter" sign on higher education, barring any further corporate encroachment. The nation's universities—one of America's most prized achievements—are where they don't belong. We do not need for-profit police or for-profit firefighters; nor do we need for-profit universities. Like the contradictory term, "alternative facts," "for-profit university" is an oxymoron.

At their best, the nation's universities represent the finest and noblest qualities—serious scholarship, investigative research, and deep learning—properties prized for their own sake, not for what you can take to the bank. The for-profit industry exhibits none of these treasured attributes. Instead, they dishonor higher education's socially responsible participation in the nation's life with fraud, greed, and theft.

It's time to roll back the corporate invasion. The Obama administration successfully closed down hundreds of predatory for-profits. Let's finish the job and shut them all down.

Targeting Low-Income Students

In her first nineteen months as U.S. Secretary of Education, Betsy DeVos issued a rush of announcements that remove or undermine previous rules designed to protect students from predatory corporate-run colleges and student debt-collection agencies—changes that are likely to impact low-income students disproportionately (Press, 2018).

DeVos' actions call to mind a dark moment in American history when the fox was guarding the henhouse: the Teapot Dome Scandal, when Harding administration cabinet members lined their pockets with public money, leasing government property to private interests. The lesson from that era is surely that it is unwise to appoint corporate insiders to regulate their own industry.

In one of her worst announcements, DeVos signed a deal worth hundreds of millions of dollars with Windham Professionals, Inc., a company with which she recently had financial ties (Douglas-Gabriel, 2018). Windham is one of two firms selected by the Education Department to help the government collect overdue student loans.

Windham and Performant Financial Corp. won out over forty others for government debt-collection contracts worth up to $400 million. DeVos' investments in Windham were sold a hair's breadth before she became education secretary—divesting them along with 107 other business ventures that smacked of conflict of interest.

She also led a campaign to keep the for-profit-friendly Accrediting Council for Independent Colleges and Schools (ACICS) alive. DeVos reinstated it over findings by her own department that it failed to meet 57 of 93 criteria required under federal law (Kreighbaum, 2018). ACICS had approved the for-profit chains ITT Technical Institute and Corinthian Colleges, which faced a series of legal challenges over their practices and are now out of business.

DeVos' department issued new, narrowly restrictive guidelines that pull teeth out of Obama-era "borrowers defense to repayment" rules. The revised rules set the bar so high that it was altogether futile for students defrauded by for-profit education providers to get their loans forgiven. Poorly served students will now be eligible for relief only if they can prove they were deliberately misled. Since 2015, the Education Department has received more than a hundred thousand fraud claims, with most still under review. The DeVos proposal also permits schools to force students to sign arbitration agreements, barring them from suing—a practice that favors for-profits.

In perhaps her most troubling action, DeVos scrapped the so-called "gainful employment" rule, a regulation that would have required for-profit colleges to prove that enrolled students can earn a decent living after graduation. According to *The New York Times*, it was "the most drastic in a series of policy shifts that will free the scandal-scarred, for-profit sector from safeguards put in effect during the Obama era."

The rule would have cut off federal funds and access to financial aid for poorly performing schools. In another action—never announced officially by

136 Problems and Considerations

the Education Department—DeVos disbanded a team at the agency looking into widespread for-profit abuse. "The unwinding of the team has effectively killed investigations into possibly fraudulent activities at several large for-profit colleges where top hires of Betsy DeVos, the education secretary, had previously worked," *The Times* concluded (Ivory et al., 2018).

DeVos' moves become clearer when you look at who DeVos has brought into the department during her tenure.

Julian Schmoke, Jr. leads the unit that polices fraud in higher education. Schmoke previously directed campus operations at the for-profit West Georgia Technical College and served as a dean at DeVry University. DeVry's parent, now rebranded as Adtalem Global Education, last year paid the Federal Trade Commission $100 million in fines for misleading students about potential decent-paying jobs after graduation. Separately, the company settled with the Education Department over similar serious allegations. Schmoke is also responsible for processing student debt relief for defrauded students (Stratford, 2017).

Robert Eitel, a former vice president at two for-profit operators, Bridgepoint Education and Career Education Corp., played a decisive role in suspending the "borrower defense to repayment" rules. According to ABC News, Eitel circulated talking points opposing borrower defense to department staff, edited documents, and even signed off on a public delay notice. Last year, Bridgepoint reached a $23.5 million settlement with the Consumer Financial Protection Bureau to refund defrauded students and pay an $8 million civil penalty for deceiving them (Dooley, 2018).

Two hundred years ago, Thomas Jefferson, perhaps the most reflective founder of our American democracy, writing to a close French friend, outlined essentials that must guide the ethical conduct of government:

> But when we come to the moral principles on which the government is to be administered, we come to what is proper for all conditions of society . . . Liberty, truth, probity, honor, are declared to be the four cardinal principles of your society. I believe with you that morality, compassion, generosity, are innate elements of the human constitution.
> (Jefferson, 1816)

In running a kleptocracy out of the Department of Education, Betsy DeVos turned her back on Jefferson's notion of responsible and dedicated government.

REFERENCES

Brown, M. (2017). Donald Trump and Betsy DeVos Survey and Report. *Lenedu.*

Carey, K. (2017, June 30). DeVos Is Discarding College Policies That New Evidence Shows Are Effective. *New York Times.*

Cellini, S. R. (2020, November 2). *The alarming rise in for-profit college enrollment.* Retrieved from https://www.brookings.edu/blog/brown-center-chalkboard/2020/11/02/the-alarming-rise-in-for-profit-college-enrollment/

Dooley, E. (2018, May 15). Former For-profit College Executive Shaped Education Department Policy That Could Benefit Former Employers. *ABC News.*

Douglas-Gabriel, D. (2018, January 12). Education Dept. Awards Debt-Collection Contract to Company with Ties to DeVos. *Washington Post.*

Ivory, D. et al. (2018, May 13). Education Department Unwinds Unit Investigating Fraud at For-Profits. *New York Times.*

Jefferson, Thomas. (1816, April 24). To P. S. Dupont de Nemours Poplar Forest. *American History from Revolution to Reconstruction and Beyond.* Retrieved from www.let.rug.nl/usa

Kreighbaum, A. (2018, August 20). DeVos Again Delays Decision on For-Profit Accreditor. *Inside Higher Ed.*

Looney, A. and C. Yannelis. (2015). *A Crisis in Student Loans?* Washington, DC: Brookings Institution.

Mayotte, B. (2015, July 8). What the New Gainful Employment Rule Means for College Students. *U.S. News & World Report.* Retrieved from www.usnews.com/education/blogs/student-loan-ranger/2015/07/08/what-the-new-gainful-employment-rule-means-for-college-students

Press, A. (2018, July 25). Betsy DeVos Proposes Rules That Would Cut Student Loan Relief by an Estimated $13 Billion. *Los Angeles Times.*

Sharp, R. V. et al. (2017). Who Attends For-Profit Institutions? The Enrollment Landscape. In T. M. Cottom and W. A. Darity (Eds.), *For-profit Universities.* London: Palgrave Macmillan.

Simon, S. and C. Emma. (2014, March 13). Obama Hampers For-Profit Colleges. *Politico.*

Stratford, M. (2017, August 30). Trump Administration Selects Former DeVry Official to Lead College Enforcement Unit. *New York Times.*

Surowiecki, J. (2015, October 26). The Rise and Fall of For-Profit Schools. *The New Yorker.*

12

Accreditation Works

Several years ago, I spent four enlightening, engaging, intimate, collaborative, debate-filled, and exhausting days as a member of a team at a nearby university. It wasn't my first. Impulsively, I had agreed to participate in five others over twenty years at modest and grand institutions—some with deep pockets, others hanging by a thread; some with meager enrollments, others with tens of thousands—but all required to go through it. All forced to run an academic marathon every ten years, hoping at the finish line to get a thumbs-up by one of the seven U.S. regional bodies, concluding that your school has been anointed, censured, or, rarely, denied the laurel crown of accreditation.

Regional accreditation is a really big deal. It's the gold standard guarantee that a school can announce on its website to students and their families that it clinched its final exam. Once a higher education institution is accredited, students can enroll with confidence, unafraid it will suddenly fold or be revealed as just another scam, a shabby diploma mill. It assures the public that universities and colleges are legitimate, so reliable that the federal government recognizes them as worthy enough for enrolled students to receive U.S.-backed grants and loans. While institutions enter into accreditation voluntarily, without it, Uncle Sam won't give you a nickel to go to college there.

Our team's credentials were not at all shabby. The team included the president of a high-profile university, the provost of another notable school,

138

distinguished professors, and other reputable scholars and top staff drawn from highly ranked colleges and universities, public and private. While most of us were from nearby schools within an hour or two, one flew in all the way from California. Impressively, their specialties covered every aspect of university life—accounting, finance, and data analysis; curriculum, instructional technology, and course design; and assessment, accreditation, institutional effectiveness, governance, planning, and student affairs. A serious group with solid experience, no less than any of my previous teams.

Our chair, the president of a peer university, mused aloud over dinner one night, "I feel it's my obligation to serve. Other presidents take the time to visit my school. I feel I must do the same."

Evenings in our hotel conference room, the nine of us—five women and four men—would sit, hunched over our black laptops around a long table, writing our reports like graduate students in a library. Sometimes the room was so still, except for the clacking of keyboards, you'd think we were writing our dissertations. Together for four days, in classrooms, over meals, during interviews, engaging in our deliberations, we grew very close to each other, similar to a time long ago on a vacation in the Caribbean over a long weekend, when I became fast friends with others lounging on the beach—but this time without surf and palm trees. The feeling of closeness bound us together, not only this time, but at all my previous team evaluations.

Months before our visit, a thick packet of brochures, documents, and reports arrived on my desk. Inside, the principal item was the university's self-study report, a dense, 174-page, spiral-bound book, wrapped in a glossy, clear plastic cover, adorned with a montage of color photos of campus. One showed a young woman wearing blue rubber gloves, performing an experiment under a lab hood. Another depicted a romantic, snow-covered scene, framed by an antique iron gate; a very dignified classic college bell tower stood under a moonlit sky in the distance. Placed in the center of the report was the school's shield and logo. A digital version arrived separately by email.

During my visit to campus, I overheard a faculty member say that the self-study took the school three years to compile. Together with the regional commission's standards for accreditation and requirements of affiliation, the self-study formed the basis of our team's on-campus evaluation. Representing the institution's own assessment of its programs and services, positive and problematic—a unique higher education intellectual exercise, not performed anywhere outside the U.S.—it focused especially on student learning and achievement, a relatively recent emphasis in response to public criticism that higher education is failing to educate its students effectively.

140 Problems and Considerations

Flipping through the report, I came upon dozens of single-spaced pages, illustrated with colorful charts and graphs. One showed a series of stacked boxes calling out the school's "aspiration," "strategic priorities," and other key goals. In an email, soon after the document arrived, we were asked to read the report carefully, making notes in the margins about themes we may not have understood or items that may have concerned us. Like facing a mirror, the self-study is a close-up. Looking outside the frame, the team has a wider view.

We were then asked to propose names of faculty and staff or chiefs of particular academic departments or services, say, the head of athletics, or in my specialty, online learning, to flesh out the text with questions we would raise during interviews. We were also encouraged to ask for a deeper dive into data, asking for additional evidence to get a better feel for what may not have been fully illuminated by the text. For example, I asked for data on online enrollment, retention, and graduation rates.

On the evening before we were to meet with assembled university faculty and staff, we were asked to draft reports on what we learned from the self-study, deciding what we thought before we ran the gauntlet of interviews with faculty, staff, and students. In advance of engaging with the university community, we were to reveal what we felt, what we needed to note, what we might conclude, which things could be applauded as significant accomplishments, what matters could be assigned as a recommendation or suggestion, and which features must be attended to as requirements.

Interviews tested our initial insights against what we learned. Among other groups, I participated in Q&As with trustees, medical school officials, faculty, and students. Colleagues—not detectives—we weren't out to grill them, but to help guide them. Students were the most rewarding and most exciting.

To our surprise, we discovered that the conclusions reached in the self-study lacked a full-throated acknowledgment of the school's impressive successes. We also uncovered blind spots we needed to call to their attention.

In our deliberations over what we might conclude, our team shifted between judging the school's past performance on the one hand and recognizing on the other that teaching, learning, and associated support services are constantly emerging, like headlights beaming out of a tunnel. In the end, we withheld certainty in favor of offering suggestions for improvement. Wisdom won out over discipline.

"Accreditation teams are being asked to make an argument that assures academic peers and the public about current and near-term promise," remarked Daniel J. Royer in a recent paper (Royer, 2017). "They are not being asked to give an award or make a judgment related to past achievement or failures."

Unhappiness with the state of American higher education—poor student learning, rising college costs, serious student loan indebtedness, and lack of workforce preparation, among other troubles—often leads observers on the right and left to propose alternatives, some so severe they call for shutting down regional accreditors in favor of imposing state or federal rules, moving toward increased bureaucratization and compliance, snuffing out the democratic spirit that animates the system.

Unwisely, critics blame the blameless, pointing a finger at regional accreditation, rather than recognizing serious social dysfunction outside the gates of the university—economic inequality and racism—that deeply trouble many of our vulnerable students. Disturbingly, our team learned about homeless students going hungry and how the institution struggles to find ways to care for them.

Going back to late nineteenth century, regional accreditation in the U.S. is an uncommon practice. The U.S. is the only country in the world that engages institutions in their own scrutiny. In Europe, Asia, and elsewhere, ministries of education and similar government agencies are solely responsible. Some call the American way an exercise in "deliberative" democracy, an idea that reaches as far back as Aristotle, contending that scholars, together with their peers, are the most competent judges of academic quality.

On our final morning—ready for departure, our suitcases stacked in the corner of a large assembly hall—our team chair stood at a lectern facing about a hundred or so senior staff and faculty. Solemnly, the president of the university was seated in the front row.

In a relaxed and friendly talk that lasted no more than five or ten minutes, our chair smiled, announcing that everything was just fine. Our report would recommend, happily, that the school fulfilled the requirements of regional accreditation. Complimenting the assembled on having done a fine job—so good, in fact, he said that our report praised the school on achieving five major accomplishments—he noted that our team also found a number of recommendations and suggestions that they should take in the collegial spirit in which they were offered. You could feel the tension easing out of the room, like a puffed-up cushion deflating as you take your seat.

Later, when the faculty and staff dive into our report, after the regional commission approved it, they found not just a handful but dozens of proposals for improvement, some responding respectfully to their needs; others it would do well for them to take very seriously. Like good friends, we didn't tell them only what they wanted to hear; we also told them things that must

Problems and Considerations

be said. Many of our recommendations supported changes for improvement that they had insightfully and revealingly proposed themselves in their self-study, a confident result of deliberative academic democracy.

At its best, the American style of accreditation, while recognizing the government's interest in it, does not act as a police force, demanding compliance. Instead, regional accreditation, just like the members of our team, enters into a dialogue with faculty and staff in a collaborative effort to raise the bar of American higher education.

REFERENCE

Royer, D. (2017, April 25). Rhetorical Styles in University Accreditation: Judgmental Rules or Collaborative Creation? *American Journal of Economics and Sociology*, 76.

Section 5
Changing My Mind

13
Changing My Mind

RECONSIDERING MOOCS

My first reaction to MOOCs—online courses delivered worldwide over the internet to millions—was largely dismissive, since they replicated the exhausted and exhausting academic lecture, with faculty going on while students drowsily watch videos at home or elsewhere. Unimpressed, even as millions logged on, I concluded that MOOCs delivered the same tired lecture online as faculty had delivered to passive students on campus for millennia.

"The lecture in-person is just an on-campus MOOC," I noted in the *Observer* in 2015, not long after MOOCs emerged as a sensation, with a hundred and sixty thousand enrolled in a single class. "They're both ancient in style," I scorned (Smith, 2015).

In 2011, when Stanford computer scientists Sebastian Thrun and Peter Norvig streamed their robotics lectures over the internet, it made front-page news because they had astonished everyone, with MOOCs eventually attracting millions online; but they had not achieved anything really new in education, other than immense digital distribution (see Chapter 7).

Only on reflection did it occur to me that MOOCs were not so much in the business of innovative pedagogical practices, but in delivering a new form of mass education, following earlier movements to extend social

145

146 Changing My Mind

capital to greater numbers other than only those well off enough to attend Yale and Harvard and other elite colleges.

MOOCs represent the latest in the broadest global expansion of higher learning since the middle of the nineteenth century. Today, about two hundred million are enrolled in post-secondary education worldwide, up from nearly ninety million as recently as 1998 (Word Bank, 2017). Like other astonishing numbers generated in the digital era, ironically, it took eight centuries, since the founding of the University of Bologna in the eleventh century, the oldest university in Europe and one of the oldest in the world, for all of higher education throughout the world to enroll two hundred million students, while MOOCs, launched only lately, as recently as 2012, exceeding a hundred million in eight years (Shah, 2020c).

Recognizing the national interest in extending college education beyond the lucky few, in 1862, President Lincoln signed the Morrill Act, establishing the land-grant system of colleges, funded by a federal-state alliance that at first set up eighteen state colleges. Eventually, sixteen historically black colleges joined the system. Today, 1.7 million study in 109 land-grant universities, including MIT and Berkeley, in every state, U.S. territory, and the District of Columbia (Croft, 2019). Since the emergence of land-grant schools, other trends, including the passage of the GI Bill in 1944, supporting veterans returning home from World War II, accelerated the student population in the nation's universities.

My own college life owes its beginnings to a similar movement in New York City, with the launch of the city's first public college, the Free Academy in 1847, now the City University of New York, with half a million in twenty-five campuses—one of which is Brooklyn College, where students, mostly from immigrant families, until recently attended free, as I did in the nineteen-fifties (Matos Rodriquez, 2020).

Similar unprecedented increases in higher education occurred in continental Europe and Great Britain in the nineteen-sixties with the privileged giving way to greater numbers, opening a relatively closed academic world. One of the most dramatic examples is the U.K.'s Open University, with more than a hundred and twenty thousand enrolled today, including ten thousand abroad, mostly in distance courses (Open University, 2020). Established in 1969, it is the largest academic institution in the U.K. and one of the biggest in Europe. Since it was founded, more than two million have studied there.

Just as in the U.S., as industrialization leaped ahead in the middle of the nineteenth century, demand for a highly skilled workforce moved rapidly in parallel, so too recently in China, higher education mushroomed as the country's economy advanced rapidly in the nineteen-sixties through the nineteen-nineties, with millions deserting farms to work in the nation's booming factories. Today in China, more than thirty million study in the country's colleges and universities, including about half a million foreign students. Total enrollment in higher education in China accelerated aggressively from less than ten percent in the late nineteen-nineties to more than fifty percent today (Textor, 2020), transforming a vast, impoverished peasant society into a largely middle-income country today—the world's second biggest economy.

"The global trends are so strong that developing countries now have higher enrollment rates than European countries did only a few decades ago," observed Evan Schofer of the University of Minnesota and John W. Meyer at Stanford in a report on the global expansion of higher education (Schofer and Meyer, 2005).

Of course, the chief difference between those who study in colleges and universities and others who sign up for MOOCs is that with MOOCs there is no barrier to entry. To be admitted to a degree-granting program at any accredited college, students must be qualified, while MOOC learners need only log-on without any previous academic credentials. To access a MOOC, learners need not show evidence of prior learning before taking their virtual seats in front of their screens. The only qualification is desire. MOOCs, and similar new digital learning ventures, have unlocked centuries-long sealed gates to higher learning, making digital knowledge accessible to anyone with even passing curiosity.

Later, when entry fees became required for many courses and when credentials were added to earn a MOOC degree in partnership with established universities, MOOCs pivoted from the spontaneity of their early days and behaved more like conventional institutions. But even now, other than fee-based courses and accredited degrees, anyone can enter a free MOOC, merely by clicking-on.

Today, as U.S. conventional education enrollment has been slipping disconcertingly and as the pandemic continued to push away new recruits, in a surprise turnabout, MOOCs rose markedly, just at the moment when on-campus college enrollment stumbled. In a high jump, the top three MOOC providers—Coursera, edX, and FutureLearn—signed-up as many new learners in April 2020 as in the whole of the previous year. And while MOOC growth had slowed recently, response in the pandemic quickly reversed the slippage, with about thirty percent of total users signing-on during the crisis. Coursera added its greatest number of new users, with thirty-five million pouring in during the period between mid-March and the end of July 2020 (Shah, 2020b).

With most MOOC learners having already earned undergraduate degrees before logging-on to a MOOC, the MOOC marketplace benefited considerably from the enormous growth in the vast global college-educated population. To everyone's surprise, University of Pennsylvania researchers found that more than eighty percent of MOOC users already had undergrad degrees and more than forty percent had some graduate education, too, exhibiting the same pattern equally in the U.S. as elsewhere—Brazil, China, India, and South Africa—where MOOCs are quite popular (Daly, 2013).

With knowledge of new, state-of-the-art fields now decisive in technology and business, getting a jump on the latest technical fashion can move workers quickly up the ladder. Luckily for MOOCs, a good part of their inventory is in current science and technology know-how—artificial intelligence, data science, machine learning, and so on—fields that have beguiled millions to consume the latest from more than sixteen thousand courses (Shah, 2020a). For clever techies, MOOCs are the new post-graduate finishing school.

When upstart MOOCs first entered into partnerships with highly selective schools—like Berkeley, Stanford, Princeton, and others—it seemed like a dubious marriage of convenience, with academic gentry coupling with online rising stars in relationships built more on wishful than deep thinking. But like many surprising matches in life, where the partners look unsuitable, things actually worked out far better than anyone imagined. By now, eight years after the first colleges tied the knot, nearly a thousand other schools have followed (Shah, 2020a), with some entering into even more serious commitments—the most unexpected unions giving birth to nearly seventy MOOC online graduate degrees (Shah, 2020c). At the nuptials, no one could have predicted that these precarious marriages would produce so many families of thriving digital degrees from some of the world's top universities (see Chapter 7).

ONLINE IS NOT ONE THING

If you wander into face-to-face classes, say, at Brooklyn College, my alma mater, you'll find lecture halls, intricate science labs, art history classes with giant screens, and molecular biology courses, each with instructors teaching in as many ways as there are personalities and disciplines. Some of what goes on can be exciting, even thrilling. Elsewhere, not so much, with droning lectures and dreary slides. An instructor in a class down a long corridor can be as different from another teaching in the next classroom as across the nation or in a distant country. At U.S. colleges, multiplicity and difference is the accepted norm in higher education and one of its admirable distinctions.

So, too, is there multiplicity in online instruction—perhaps even more so, with many classes streamed as if on Netflix without live communication, while others are taught with faculty stimulating student engagement in real time. Still others offer hybrid delivery, with some of this and some of that, as in a lively digital and analog salad.

Looking back, I was not so accepting. When I first entered digital education at the turn of this century, I held a fixed idea of online instruction. Streaming videos, without faculty-student interaction, seemed like a bad idea, so misguided that I dismissed them altogether as unworthy of being called online learning.

Back then, digital instruction consisted almost entirely of asynchronous engagement, with students and faculty interacting with one another using on-screen bulletin boards and posting threaded discussions, with messages and replies commonly grouped together as in a layer cake, similar to text messaging today. Owing to the internet and its various ingenious applications, instructors and learners were able to communicate with one another totally apart, located neither in the same place nor seated in class at the same time. Routinely facilitated by course management systems, learners interacted with one another, as well as faculty, using email, wikis, blogs, electronic mailing lists, and related asynchronous tools. It was one of the most rewarding academic technical achievements in this century.

Once internet access at high speeds and broad bandwidth became largely available universally, vast new opportunities opened for online learning in real time, with video streaming, videoconferencing systems, and other synchronous communication options. During the 2020 pandemic, higher education would surely have shut down were it not for Zoom and its video-conferencing cousins (see Chapter 1).

In an article I wrote about twenty years ago in *IEEE Spectrum*, "Engineers Turn to eLearning," (Ubell, 2000), I was so doctrinaire in what I allowed as virtual instruction, that in a list I had assembled of engineering schools delivering online degrees, I deliberately excluded Columbia University's notable online engineering master's degrees—applauded at the top of *U.S. News & World Report* rankings of online master's programs—because courses in the Columbia program were all videostreamed, a form of delivery that failed to meet my standards of what constituted true online education, with students set in front of computer screens, passively watching lessons stream by, instead of faculty and students engaging actively with one another. It was a harsh judgement. In this book, too, the chapter on "Theory and Practice" captures my preoccupation with active learning as the most privileged of diverse virtual instruction practices (see Chapter 2).

150 Changing My Mind

It was a failure of vision, so narrow that it allowed in only those elected as members of my exclusive online club for which I was the sole gatekeeper.

These revisionist thoughts were prompted by a long weekend spent in the country, away from my city apartment during the recent pandemic. Looking out across the landscape one afternoon, I was struck suddenly by the immeasurable variety in nature—all sorts of trees were spread out before me, a myriad of shapes and heights; gnarled and twisted trunks; tall, thin, elegant branches; pines, still green in winter while most trees were bare; and others too numerous to list. Even looking at a single variety, the differences displayed by one from the other were incalculably varied.

At home, I was drawing close to the end of my manuscript for this book, thinking about this chapter, covering how I had changed my mind about online learning since my early days in digital education a couple of decades ago. With the measureless display of nature massed before me, it brought to mind my own constraints, how trapped I was by the limits I had imposed. How stunningly beautiful it was out there in the sweep of nature; how pinched my view was of what constituted online learning. High time to open up.

And so, I went back to my *IEEE Spectrum* article in my thoughts and apologized, *sotto voce*, to Columbia for being so mean-spirited. I now aimed to open my exclusive online club to the immense variety of digital instruction practices.

If you hop online, looking to enroll in a virtual degree-granting program today, you'll find a great variety of options—with thousands of choices available in synchronous, asynchronous, and blended (or hybrid) modes. Among schools offering blended courses, you're likely to find programs that offer *flipped classrooms* as an instruction strategy (Bergmann and Sams, 2012), with students reading assignments or watching videos at home or in their dorm rooms, then moving online to participate in virtual discussions in real time together with their instructor and online classmates, similar to the way I ran my New School course a few years ago (see Chapter 2).

In a flipped classroom, learning shifts from the instructor to the student in what is known as learner-centered pedagogy, in which online classroom time is devoted to examining topics that students explored offline on their own, before interacting collaboratively in class afterward. In conventional instruction, the teacher occupies the center, delivering lectures and feeding students with questions about the content the instructor conveyed. Pioneered by Colorado high school teacher Jon Bergmann, flipped classrooms encourage faculty to move from the center to the periphery as a guide or mentor, giving students freedom to acquire knowledge and evaluate their success on their own and in concert with their peers.

In an another relatively new alternative to conventional instruction, *HyFlex* (also known as hybrid-flexible course design), gives students access to a rare mix of choices, combining face-to-face with online instruction. Originated at San Francisco State University, HyFlex classes are offered in-person, but in a unique departure, they are paired with synchronous and asynchronous online delivery (Beatty, 2019). Often implemented for non-traditional learners, in the HyFlex model, an instructor is available on campus for face-to-face support if needed, while students study independently online or join their classmates in group projects. Students learn individually on a customized, fluid schedule, choosing to come to class on campus or go online, flexibly selecting the practice that suits them best. They are free to come and go on and off campus as they wish, as students often conduct themselves at Oxford and Cambridge. Meeting in person may vary from one implementation to the next, with some classes held face-to-face daily, while others provide little on-campus instruction.

Perhaps the most effective and richest exercise of blended learning is the inventive introduction of asynchronous and synchronous modes, adopting the incredible array of applications as course content and pedagogy require. Like a good cook, the skilled virtual instructor flavors online recipes with an amazing variety of digital ingredients, from brief instructional videos to keyboard activities that activate digital learning games, not only exploiting digital tools, but also the immense conventional print literature, like a bountiful chef, consulting cookbooks to enrich the character of what's on the academic menu.

For a time, online scholars debated the benefits and constraints of asynchronous *versus* synchronous instruction, seeking to uncover which works best, but like my new, more eclectic appreciation of digital education delivery modes, the argument has lost its force, with most practitioners concluding that each has its own merits, accepting that neither one nor the other is best.

REFERENCES

Beatty, B. J. (Ed.). (2019). *Hybrid-Flexible Course Design*. EdTech Books. Retrieved from https://edtechbooks.org/hyflex

Bergmann, J. and A. Sams. (2012). Flip Your Classroom: Reach Every Student in Every Class Every Day. Washington, DC: ISTE and ASCD.

Croft, G. K. (2019). *The U.S. Land-Grant University System*. Washington, DC: Congressional Research Service.

152   Changing My Mind

Daly, J. (2013, December 4). 80 Percent of MOOC Students Already Have a College Degree. *EdTech*.

Matos Rodriquez, F. V. (2020). *The CUNY Story: A Brief History*. Retrieved December 19, 2020, from www.cuny.edu/about/history/

Open University. (2020, December 12). *The World's Leading Distance-learning Provider*. London: The Open University.

Schofer, E. and J. M. Meyer. (2005, December). The Worldwide Expansion of Higher Education in the Twentieth Century. *American Sociological Review*, 70, 898–920.

Shah, D. (2020a, August 16). By the Numbers: MOOCs During the Pandemic. *Class Central*. Retrieved from https://www.classcentral.com/report/mooc-stats-pandemic/

Shah, D. (2020b, November 30). By the Numbers: MOOCs in 2020. *Class Central*. Retrieved from https://www.classcentral.com/report/mooc-stats-2020/

Shah, D. (2020c, December 7). Coursera's 2020: Year in Review. *Class Central*. Retrieved from https://www.classcentral.com/report/coursera-2020-year-review/

Smith, J. (2015, January 21). Free Online Courses Are Still Falling Short of Their Ultimate Promise. *Observer*.

Textor, C. (2020, November 9). Number of Public Colleges and Universities in China Between 2009 and 2019. *Statista*.

Ubell, R. (2000, October). Engineers Turn to e-Learning. *IEEE Spectrum*.

Word Bank. (2017, October 5). *Higher Education*. The World Bank. Retrieved from www.worldbank.org/en/topic/tertiaryeducation#:~:text=Today%2C%20 there%20are%20around%20200,doubled%20in%20the%20past%20decade

Index

2U 81, 85–86

Absent-Minded Professor, The (movie) 83
academic bureaucracy 102
academic calendar 36, 121
accreditation teams 138–142
Accrediting Council for Independent Colleges and Schools (ACICS) 135
ACICS *see* Accrediting Council for Independent Colleges and Schools (ACICS)
Acrobatiq 43
active-learning 18, 24, 96–97, 111; benefits of 6, 26, 46, 59; challenges 25; student-centered 55
adaptive learning 42; failures as success 44–47; mergers and acquisitions 43–44
ADDIE (Analysis, Design, Development, Implementation, and Evaluation) framework 24
adjunct instruction 52–53
Ahearn, Amy 94–95
ALEKS software 43–44
Alexander, Bryan 93
Amazon 53, 122
Arizona State University (ASU) 36, 62, 121–122
Arkansas State University 65
Arum, Richard 20, 22
authoring software 23
automated quiz 96–97

Baker, Nelson 52, 67, 102
Bates, Tony 71
behaviorism 27
Bellantuono, Lisa 36–37, 118–119
Bergmann, Jon 150–151

Berklee College of Music 66
Berra, Yogi 8, 25
Biden, Joe 103
Bidjerano, Temi 33
blended learning 60–62, 108, 150
Bloomberg, Michael 65
Bol, Peter 86
borrower-defense rule 133–135
Branbery, Stuart 62
Brand, Steward 103
Brewer, Dominic 85
Brooklyn College 121, 146, 148
Brown University 65
Bruner, Jerome 25
Byrne, Michelle M. 19

Campus Computing Survey 42
Carey, Kevin 134
Carnegie Learning 43
cheating, online 127–130
Chen, Zhenghao 45–47
chief information officers (CIOs) 42
China 108; higher education in 147; internet censorship in 110–111; MOOCs in 116; online experience in 109–110
Christensen, Clayton 56–57
Chronicle of Higher Education, The 26
classrooms: conventional 11, 27, 128; flipped 24, 73, 150; virtual 34, 57, 60
colleges/universities: closures of 55; declining tuition fees 68; for-profit 131–132
Columbia University 33, 65, 149
communication: asynchronous/synchronous 28, 149; technologies 22
community colleges, virtual instruction at 33
constructivism 25–30

153

154 Index

content libraries 44
convenience, in online learning 119–123
Corinthian University 133–134
Cormier, Dave 93
corporate consolidation 43
Coursera 45–47, 62, 66, 98, 147; completion rates 95; Coursera Labs 97; Coursera Specialization 105; credit-bearing degrees 101; Guided Projects 97; profit 98
COVID-19 pandemic: affecting higher education 56; decline in international students 114; greater enrollment 62; online classes after 3
Craig, Ryan 12, 30, 120
critical mass 74–76
Crow, Michael M. 62–63
Cuomo, Andrew 102
customer-centric service 120

Darwin, Charles 82, 84
D'Aunno, Thomas 87
demand, and supply 59–60
Designing Online Learning Programs 6
DeVos, Betsy 133–136
DeVry University 136
Dewey, John 6, 25, 27, 45, 54
digital courses 6, 36, 59; cost of 70, 72; unprepared faculty members 8, 22
digital currency 82
digital degrees 67, 72, 102, 148
digital economy, academic 59, 83; blended learning 60–62; critical mass 74–76; declining college tuition fees 68; digital recruitment 62–63; infrastructure/marketing investments 53–55; online costs 70–72; scaling-up 55–59; small colleges 68–70; students/faculty 52–53; supply and demand 59–60; tuition strategies 63–68
digital education 4–5, 9; blended courses 62; evolution of 23–24, 74
digital learning 12, 28, 38, 151
digital marketing 29, 62, 85, 133
digital recruitment 62–63, 90

digital skills 23
digital students 35, 51
digital technologies 83; *see also* technology(ies)
digital transformation, of higher education 23
DiPaolo, Andy 73
disruptive innovation 56–57
distance education courses 58
division-of-labor approach 117
Downes, Stephen 93
Duckworth, Angela 46
Ducoff, Nick 56
Duke Learning Innovation 6, 12
Duncan, Arne 133

Ebbinghaus, Hermann 129
École Normale Supérieure, Yale 99
EdAssist 104
Edmit 56
education: conventional 8, 147; for-profit 131–132, 134; progressive 6, 54; technology-enhanced 84; virtual 54; *see also* digital education; digital learning; e-learning; higher education; online learning
edX 66, 80–81, 97, 147; completion rates 95; discounts 101; profit 98
Eitel, Robert S. 134, 136
Ekman, Richard 69
e-learning 104–105
El-Sadr, Wafaa 8
Engageli 99
Essa, Alfred 42
EvoLLLution magazine 58

face-to-face instruction 8, 18–19, 33, 51, 148
faculty: anxiety 21, 28; authority of 115; different 52–53; helping at-risk students 119; resistance to online instruction 59; teaching online 52; training 10
failures: success through 44–47; in U.S. higher education 20
Ferreira, Jose 44
Fishtree 43

Fitzgerald, Susan 55
flipped classrooms 24, 73, 150
for-profit education 131–132, 134
Fredericksen, Eric 75
Freeman, Scott 96
Freire, Paulo 6, 25, 54, 128
FutureLearn 147

gainful employment rule 133, 135
Gartner hype cycle 43
Gates, Bill 44
Georgia Tech 67
Goffman, Erving 19
Going Online (Ubell) 22, 66
Gonick, Lev 121
Google Meet 5
Google Scholar 74
Grappo, Rebecca 113
group discussions 23
Grove, Andy 59
guanxi 115
Guided Projects (Coursera) 97

Hartman, Joel 60–61
Harvard University 83, 86
higher education: digital transformation of 23; disruptive innovation 56–57; failures in U.S. 20; market forces 58; withdrawal of 55
Hill, Phil 3, 43, 74, 85, 96, 99
holistic strategy, for online education 118–119
Holon IQ 86
Horn, Michael 62
HotChalk 85
hybrid learning *see* blended learning
HyFlex (hybrid-flexible course design) 73, 151

infrastructure, virtual 9, 53–55
Inside Higher Ed 18, 70
Institute of International Education 113
instructional design 21–25, 35
Integrated Postsecondary Education Data System (IPEDS) 61
intelligent tutoring systems 43

international (foreign) students 112–116
internet marketing 62
internet service, lack of 4
involvement shields 20
IPEDS *see* Integrated Postsecondary Education Data System (IPEDS)
Iron Triangle 63
Ithaka S+R 20
Ivy League 100

Jacobsohn, Ilan 11, 17, 24, 29, 85
Jefferson, Thomas 136
Johns Hopkins University 65
Jupiter Notebook 97

Karr, Jane 56
Kim, Joshua 55, 90
Knewton 43, 44
knowledge 26–27, 89; demonstrating 23; digital 147; freedom to acquire 151; of online learning 96, 109
Knowre 43
Koller, Daphne 47, 99

learning: active 18, 24, 96–97, 111; adaptive 42; blended 60–62, 108, 150; digital 12, 28, 38, 151; peer-to-peer 27, 59; remote 10, 12, 35; web-based distance 54, 59; *see also* e-learning; online learning
Learning and the Future of Higher Education (Kim & Maloney) 55
learning management systems (LMSs) 5, 71, 76
Legon, Ron 11–12
Levin, Rick 101
Lincoln, Abraham 146
Lloyd, Steven A. 19
LMSs *see* learning management systems (LMSs)
loan forgiveness 133
low-income (poor) students 34, 101, 132; higher education for 39; targeting 134
low-stakes quizzes 128

156 Index

MacMurray, Fred 83
Maloney, Edward 55
marketing investments, different 53–55
massed practice 129
massive open online courses (MOOCs)
11, 44–46, 58, 62, 85; completion rates
of 94; into money-making machines
100; on-the-job training 103–106;
paid options 97–103; reconsidering
145–148; revolution 93–94
Mazur, Eric 26
McCoy, Tami S. 19
McCready, Peggy 120
McFarland, Scott 130
McGraw-Hill 43, 44
Memphis College of Art 55, 57
MicroMasters 101, 102
Miller, Shawn 6, 8
Mills College 64
Mintz, Steven 19
MOOCs *see* massive open online
courses (MOOCs)
Moodie, Gavin 112
Moody's Investment Service 56
Morrill Act 146

National Student Clearinghouse
Research Center 7, 63
"needle trades" 39
New School 22
Ng, Andrew 47
Nicholson, Paul 104
nonprofit institutions 55
Norvig, Peter 93, 145
NYU (New York University) 36, 64–65,
73, 88

Obama, Barrack 60
occupational labor shortage 59
online abroad 108–116; China
experience 109–110; online students
112–113; satellite campuses
110–112; students online 113–116
online campus 51
online cheating 127–130
online convenience 119–123
online costs 70–72

online courses, building and assessing
23–24
online education: as ethical practice
32–34; failure 44–47; post-industrial
economy 37–40; promises of 57;
through streaming videos 11;
supporting online students 34–37;
for underserved students 40; for
working adults 39–40
online instruction, faculty resistance
to 59
online learners, finding/keeping
117–123; convenience 119–123;
holistic alternative 118–119
online learning 5–6; as asynchronous
learning networks 54; boom in
54–55; convenience, in 119–123;
theory and practice 17; in U.S. 12
Online Learning Consortium Quality
Scorecard 23
online predators: *borrower-defense*
rule 133–134; *gainful-employment*
rule 133; hiring for-profit executives
134–136
online program managers (OPMs) 9,
62, 89
on-the-job training 103
Open University 146
OPMs *see* online program managers (OPMs)
outsourcing 80–91; *vs.* insourcing
88–91; online program management
84–88; organic growth 81–84

pandemic pedagogy 6–7
Papert, Seymour 27
peer-to-peer learning 23, 27, 59
Peking University 99
Pell grants 132
Performant Financial Corp 135
Phil on EdTech blog 43
Piaget, Jean 6, 46, 54
Pollack, Karen 59
post-industrial economy 37–40, 52
PowerPoint 19
*Proceedings of the National Academy of
Sciences* 26
ProctorU 129

Quality Matters 23
quizzes 23, 47, 96–97, 128–129

Raimondo, Gina 102
regional accreditation 138–142
remote learning 10, 12, 35
remote/virtual proctoring 129
residential students 71
Rhyme Softworks 97
Richman, Shira 22, 24, 29
Rogers, Everett 76
Roksa, Josipa 20
Roosevelt, Mark 65
Royer, Daniel J. 140
RStudio 97

Sanders, Bernie 103
satellite campuses 110–112
Saxenian, AnnaLee 86
scaling-up 55–59
Schmoke, Julian 136
Schofer, Evan 147
Schonfeld, Erick 98
Seaman, Jeff 59, 70, 75
Selingo, Jeffrey J. 18, 24
Seltzer, Rick 64
Sense 47
Sharma, Anju 4–5
Shea, Peter 28, 33, 74
skilled workers 37–38
Skinner, B.F. 27
Sloan Foundation 53–54
small colleges 68–70
SmartBook 44
Smart Sparrow 43
social risks 56
soft skills 39
spacing practice 129
sponsorship, losing 36
Stanford University 113
state funding 55–56
Stevens Institute of Technology 81, 88, 108–110, 120
St. John's University 65
Strikwerda, Carl J. 119
students: cultural immersion 108; different 52–53; engagement 20, 36;

international/foreign 112–116; loan/debt 132; services 35
study-abroad programs 111
Stukel, James J. 34
sunk costs 71
supply, and demand 59–60
Surowiecki, James 131
Swan, Karen 28, 34

"teaching presence" 28
technical demands, unprepared 36
technical inadequacy 21
technology(ies) 22, 37, 76, 100; adaptive 42; enhanced education 84; LMSs and videoconferencing 5
Tegrity 129
theory and practice: constructivism 25–30; instructional design 21–25; online learning 17
Thrun, Sebastian 93–94, 145
tuition: resets 64; strategies 63–68; tuition-free college program 103
Tyton Partners survey 18

Udacity 80, 94, 99
unemployment 7
United Kingdom (UK), academic institution in 146
United States (US): Department of Labor 37, 38; higher education in 3–4
universities, digital services in 120–121
University of Bologna 146
University of Central Florida (UCF) 61
University of Groningen 112
University of Michigan 7
University of Pennsylvania (UPenn) 66, 100, 148
University of Phoenix 60, 133
Urban, Joseph 22

Vagelos College of Physicians and Surgeons 65
videoconferencing 5–6, 149
Virginia Community College System 33
virtual alienation 36
virtual capabilities 89

158 Index

virtual classrooms 34, 57, 60
virtual dishonesty 127
virtual education 54
virtual instruction 5, 12, 33, 51, 57, 61–62, 73
virtual pedagogy 60
virtual teams 23, 27, 59
virtual tuition 67
virtual university 51
Vivolo, John 23, 81–82
VS Code 97
Vygotsky, Lev 25, 27

Wagner, Robert F. 87
Wall Street, and for-profit education 131–132
WCET research 70–71

web-based distance learning 54, 59
Webex 5
web instruction 103
Weisberg, Allan 104
Wieman, Carl 26
Windham Professionals, Inc. 135
work from home 6
working adults 34, 38–40, 60
Wu, Tim 121, 123

Xi'an Jiaotong University 111
XuetangX 98

Young, Jeffrey R. 86

Zoom 5–6, 10, 11, 149